Diasporas in Antiquity

Program in Judaic Studies
Brown University
BROWN JUDAIC STUDIES

Edited by
Ernest S. Frerichs
Shaye J. D. Cohen, Calvin Goldscheider

Number 288

Diasporas in Antiquity

edited by
Shaye J.D. Cohen
Ernest S. Frerichs

Diasporas in Antiquity

edited by
Shaye J.D. Cohen
Ernest S. Frerichs

Scholars Press
Atlanta, Georgia

Diasporas in Antiquity

edited by
Shaye J.D. Cohen
Ernest S. Frerichs

Library of Congress Cataloging-in-Publication Data

Diasporas in antiquity / edited by Shaye J. D. Cohen, Ernest S. Frerichs.
     p. cm.—(Brown Judaic studies ; no. 288)
  Includes index.
  ISBN 1-55540-918-0
  1. Jewish diaspora—Philosophy—Congresses. 2. Judaism—History—
Post-exilic period, 586 B.C.-210 A.D.—Congresses. 3. Jews—
Identity—Congresses. 4. Migrations of nations—Congresses.
5. Civilization, Ancient—Congresses. I. Cohen, Shaye J. D.
II. Frerichs, Ernest S. III. Series.
DS134.D5225 1993
930'.04924—dc20   93-37125
                                 CIP

Printed in the United States of America
on acid-free paper

Table of Contents

Preface

This book has its origin in several concerns and rests on several recognitions. The first of these was an occasion to honor Professor Shaye J. D. Cohen who was appointed by Brown University in 1991 as its first Samuel Ungerleider, Jr., Professor of Judaic Studies. Professor Cohen came to Brown University from the Jewish Theological Seminary of America where he was serving as Dean of the Graduate School, Professor of Jewish History, and Shenkman Professor of the Post-Biblical Foundations of Western Civilization. To honor Professor Cohen was to provide an opportunity for an inaugural lecture. In planning for such an occasion, we concluded that it would be desirable to place the inaugural lecture in the context of a conference examining an issue of significance in the study of not only ancient Judaism, but antiquity generally.

This concern led to the planning of a conference, Diasporas in Antiquity, held on the 30th of April, 1992. The conference took as its premise the belief that the contemporary common usage of the word "diaspora," which links the word to the experience of the Jewish people in their exile to Babylon and their dispersion throughout the Mediterranean world, is too exclusive an application. Viewed as a mass migration or movement or flight from one location to another location or locations, diaspora could be viewed as an event in the history of several peoples of antiquity. Clearly the fact of dispersion and its many consequences have been an experience of many people, ancient and modern. Major issues for investigation include the question of whether, and how, these "dispersed" peoples maintain a sense of self-identity and a measure of communal cohesion. The central question for diaspora peoples is adaptation: how to adapt to the environment without surrendering group identity. These questions faced by the diaspora communities of antiquity are still apparent in modern times.

Assembled for the conference were three scholars who would raise several perspectives on the general issue of diasporas. Professor Joseph Mélèze-Modrzejewski is the Professor of Ancient History at the Sorbonne, University of Paris I, and Professor of Papyrology and Ancient Legal History in the Ecole Pratique des Hautes Etudes, IVeme Section: Sciences Historique et Philologiques. Professor Mélèze-Modrzejewski explored the notion of diaspora and the adaptation of the Jews of Egypt to their Greco-Egyptian environment. From an issue in Egypt to an issue in Rome, Professor Ramsay MacMullen, Dunham Professor of History and Classics at Yale University, examined the ethnic Syrian communities of the city of Rome. Professor Cohen centered his attention on the issue of Jewish identity, exploring the question of how the Jews of the ancient Diaspora made themselves distinctive without making themselves conspicuous. On the recommendation of Professor Mélèze-Modrzejewski, the editors invited a French scholar, Ms. Sylvie Honigman, to contribute an essay on a related topic, the emergence of a Jewish self-definition in Ptolemaic Egypt as reflected in onomastic usage.

A further concern of the conference was to lift up the name of the man for whom the professorship is named, Samuel A. Ungerleider, Jr., and to recognize the benefactors who had made this endowed professorship possible. The man in question was a graduate of Brown in the Class of 1939 who had pursued several careers in journalism and in the executive leadership of the Central National Corporation-Gottesman, Inc. His support for Brown and his support for Judaic Studies were well established before his death in 1972. As Vice-President of the D.S.&R.H. Gottesman Foundation, Samuel Ungerleider had supported a major grant from the Gottesman Foundation in the 1960s to enable Brown to experiment with alternative directions for the development of a Judaic Studies program at Brown. Following his death the Gottesman Foundation endowed an Ungerleider Distinguished Scholar's Fund which continued until a recent benefaction enabled the University to convert that Fund into the Samuel A. Ungerleider, Jr., Professorship in Judaic Studies. The Ungerleider Professorship serves as a memorial to the late husband of Joy Ungerleider Mayerson, President of the Dorot Foundation of New York City.

This Conference volume will serve as a contribution to the study of diasporas in antiquity and a stimulus to further investigations of other ancient diasporas and their effect. It will also serve as a recognition of the Ungerleider Professorship, its generous donors and Professor Cohen as the first Ungerleider Professor. Celebrated in this Conference was a recognition of the vision of many within and without the University who dreamed and worked to give Judaic Studies a permanent role in the lives of Brown's students and faculty. We remember with abiding gratitude the contributions of all those who have made the Ungerleider Professorship and the Program in Judaic Studies possible.

Ernest S. Frerichs
Brown University

1

"Those Who Say They Are Jews and Are Not": How Do You Know a Jew in Antiquity When You See One?

Shaye J.D. Cohen

In the New Testament book of *Revelation* the risen Jesus appears in a vision to John of Patmos and instructs him to write letters to the protecting angels of the seven churches of Asia Minor. The letter to the church in Philadelphia includes the following lines:

> I know that you have but little power, and yet you have kept my word and have not denied my name. Behold, I will make those of the synagogue of Satan who say that they are Jews and are not, but lie – behold, I will make them come and bow down before your feet, and learn that I have loved you. (Revelation 3:8-9)

A similar phrase appears in the letter to the church in Smyrna ("I know your tribulation and your poverty ... and the slander by those who

This essay has been much improved by the suggestions and criticisms of David Konstan and Joseph Mélèze-Modrzejewski. I have also benefitted from several rabbinic references provided by Hebert Basser, Marc Bregman, and Ranon Katzoff.

Menachem Stern, *Greek and Latin Authors on Jews and Judaism* (3 vols.; Jerusalem: Israel Academy of Sciences and Humanities, 1974-1984) is cited throughout as "Stern." In the citation of rabbinic literature, "M." indicates Mishnah, "T." Tosefta, "Y." Yerushalmi, and "B." Bavli. In the transliteration of Greek an omega is indicated by a *w*.

say that they are Jews and are not, but are a synagogue of Satan,"
Revelation 2:9). Who are these people who say that they are Jews but are
not? The simplest and likeliest explanation is that Jews are meant.[1] The
author of Revelation believes that the title "Jew" (*Ioudaios*) is an
honorable designation and properly belongs only to those who believe in
Christ, just as Paul says that the real Jew is not the one outwardly with
circumcision in the flesh but the one inwardly with circumcision in the
heart and spirit (Romans 2:28-29; cf. Philippians 3:3).[2] It is the Jews who
are slandering and persecuting the nascent and relatively powerless
churches of Smyrna and Philadelphia, and as a result the Jews are
deemed to be "synagogues of Satan."

Christian appropriation of the name *Ioudaios* did not end in the first
century, of course. Augustine knows Christians who still call themselves
Iudaei, and the father of Hippo explains to them that Christians can and
should be called Israel, but not *Iudaei*, even though in theory this name
belongs to them as well.[3] Between the late first century, the date of
Revelation, and the late fourth or early fifth century, the period of
Augustine, the separation of Jews from Christians, and Christians from
Jews, proceeded apace, so that much that was true for Augustine of
Hippo was not true for John of Patmos (and vice versa!).[4] For Revelation

---

[1]Adela Yarbro Collins, "Insiders and Outsiders in the Book of Revelation," *"To See Ourselves as Others See Us": Christians, Jews, "Others" in Late Antiquity*, ed. Jacob Neusner and Ernest S. Frerichs (Scholars Press, 1985) 187-218, at 204-210 (an expanded version of an article that appeared in the *Harvard Theological Review* 79 [1986] 308-320, at 310-314). See 205 n. 88 for a list of scholars who argue that non-Christian Jews are meant, and 205 n. 89 for a list of scholars who argue that certain kinds of Christians are meant. Collins herself persuasively defends the first position. For a parallel note the long recension of the letters of Ignatius (probably late fourth century) which uses *pseudoioudaioi* to mean "Jews"; see J. B. Lightfoot ed., *The Apostolic Fathers: Clement Ignatius and Polycarp* part II vol. 3 (London: Macmillan 1889-1890; repr. Peabody: Hendrickson, 1989) 160 and 212.

[2]Perhaps Revelation is following the Philonic view that the name *Judah*, the progenitor of the name *Ioudaios*, means "confession of praise to God." Only those who believe in Christ confess God, and therefore only those who believe in Christ deserve the name Jew. See the Philonic passages listed by J.W. Earp in volume 10 of the Loeb edition of Philo (Cambridge: Harvard, 1962) 357 note *a*. Many church fathers followed this view; see Nicholas De Lange, *Origen and the Jews* (Cambridge: Cambridge University, 1976) 32 n. 29. Unless I am mistaken Philo nowhere associates *Ioudaios* with Judah, but we may assume that he and other first century Jews knew the connection; see Josephus *Jewish Antiquities* 11.5.7 173 and Justin, *Historiae Philippicae* 36.2.5 = Stern #137.

[3]Augustine, Epistle 196 (= *Corpus Scriptorum Ecclesiasticorum Latinorum*, v. 57 pp. 216-230).

[4]Tertullian already remarks *neque de consortio nominis cum Iudaeis agimus*, *Apology* 21:2.

Ioudaios is a theological category:[5] real *Ioudaioi* are those who believe in Christ. For Augustine *Judaeus* ought to be a theological category, but instead it is a sociological category; Christians are the true *Judaei* but will create too much confusion if they use that title. Let the Jews have it.

The striking phrase "those who say they are Jews and are not" may well have been a current expression in the first century. It will have applied originally to gentiles who "act the part of Jews" but are not in fact Jews, and was deliberately and cleverly misapplied by Revelation to the Jews themselves.[6] The phrase illustrates the ambiguities inherent in Jewish identity and "Jewishness," especially in the diaspora. In the homeland (at least until the fourth century CE) Jewishness for Jews was natural, perhaps inevitable, but in the diaspora Jewishness was a conscious choice, easily avoided or hidden, and at best tolerated by society at large. In this paper I am interested in the social dynamics of "Jewishness" in the Roman diaspora in the last century BCE and the first centuries CE. How was Jewishness expressed? What did a Jew do (or not do) in order to demonstrate that s/he was not a gentile? If someone claimed to be a Jew, how could you ascertain whether the claim was true? In sum, how did you know a Jew in antiquity when you saw one?[7]

Social mechanisms which did not make Jews distinctive

I begin with a discussion of those factors that did *not* render Jews distinctive. Many Greek and Roman authors talk about Jews and Judaism, usually focusing on those characteristics that make Jews and Judaism peculiar, different from what these authors take to be "normal."[8] It is striking to note, then, what these authors do *not* say. Not a single ancient author says that Jews are distinctive because of their looks, clothing, speech, names, or occupations. I shall now discuss each of these points.

---

[5]The word *ioudaios* appears in Revelation only in these two passages.

[6]I owe this suggestion to David Konstan. For those who "act the part of Jews" but are not in fact Jews, see the passage of Epictetus cited and discussed below.

[7]In his *Who was a Jew?* (Hoboken: Ktav, 1985), Lawrence H. Schiffman ignores these social questions entirely and focuses exclusively on the history of rabbinic law, as if rabbinic law were the only legal system in antiquity that had an interest in defining Jewishness and as if legal history were social history. In my discussion I occasionally cite rabbinic texts which, of course, derive from Palestine and/or Babylonia. These citations are entirely for the sake of confirmation, contrast or illustration; I am not interested here in the manifestations of Jewishness in Rabbinic Palestine and Babylonia.

[8]The material is easily surveyed in the three volumes of Menachem Stern, *Greek and Latin Authors on Jews and Judaism* (Jerusalem: Israel Academy of Sciences and Humanities, 1974-1984) (hereafter cited as Stern).

Not a single ancient author says that Jews are distinctive because of their looks. The Romans, and the Greeks before them, noted that foreign peoples often looked different from themselves: they were peculiarly tall or short, hairy or smooth, dark or fair. The Romans also noted peculiar styles of hair and beard.[9] But not a single ancient author comments on the distinctive size, looks, or coiffure of the Jews. The rabbis prohibited a certain type of haircut because in their estimation it was quintessentially gentile, an "Amorite custom," and in one rabbinic legend a rabbi adopts this haircut precisely in order to be able to pass as a gentile, infiltrate the councils of state, and thwart some anti-Jewish decrees; perhaps we might conclude that (some) rabbis followed this prohibition, but we surely cannot conclude that nonrabbinic Jews did.[10] In any case even the rabbis do not enjoin a distinctive Jewish hair style. Apparently Jews looked "normal." The only possible corporeal indication of Jewishness was, of course, circumcision, which I shall discuss below.[11]

Not a single ancient author says that Jews are distinctive because of their clothing. Clothing is an extension of identity. Roman clothing was distinctive, and the Roman magistrate who wore Greek clothing in public was subject to ridicule, at least in Republican times. Romans mocked the crude clothing of the northerners (Celts and Germans), while the Greeks mocked the outlandish costumes of the Persians.[12] Jewish ephebes in Hellenistic Jerusalem wore the *petasos* (2 Macc 4:12), the broad rimmed Greek hat worn by youths in the gymnasium, but no ancient author refers to a distinctively Jewish hat, or any other item of distinctively Jewish clothing.[13] Tertullian, living in Carthage at the end of the second

---

[9]J. P. V. D. Balsdon, *Romans and Aliens* (London: Duckworth, 1979) 214-219.

[10]Prohibition: T. Shabbat 6:1 p. 22 ed. Lieberman (and parallels); see the commentary of Saul Lieberman, *Tosefta Ki-Fshutah* ad loc. pp. 80-81. Legend: B. Meilah 17a.

[11]Marcus Aurelius (apud Ammianus Marcellinus, Stern #506) is said to have noted a peculiar Jewish odor or stench (*Iudaeorum fetentium*). The idea that Jews have a peculiar smell will recur frequently in the middle ages, but no one in antiquity suggests that Jews are recognizable by their odor! The notion that Jews look different (that is, different from other white Europeans) by reason of their hair, skin, face, or nose, became widespread only in the nineteenth century; see Sander L. Gilman, "The Visibility of the Jew in the Diaspora: Body Imagery and its Cultural Context" (B.G. Rudolph Lectures in Judaic Studies, Syracuse University, 1992).

[12]Balsdon 219-222.

[13]The fullest discussion remains that of Samuel Krauss, *Talmudische Archäologie* (3 vols.; Leipzig: G. Fock, 1910) 1:127-207 and *Qadmoniyot HaTalmud* (4 vols.; Tel Aviv: Dvir, 1945) 2: ; see too Jean Juster, *Les juifs dans l'empire romain* (2 vols.; Paris: Guethner, 1914) 2:215-220; E. R. Goodenough, *Jewish Symbols* (13 vols.; Princeton: Princeton University Press, 1953-1968) 9:168-174; Yigael Yadin, *Bar*

century CE, writes that Jewish women could be recognized as Jews by the fact that they wore veils in public. I think it likely, or at least plausible, that Jewish women wore veils in public in the Eastern Roman Empire, but in the Eastern Roman Empire many women wore veils in public, and Jewish women would hardly have been distinctive for doing what many other women did. Perhaps in Carthage, a western town, the veils of Jewish women made them distinctive, but I know of no other evidence for the easy recognizability of Jews, either male or female, in antiquity.[14]

Kochba (NY: Random House, 1971) 66-85 (note especially 69, "The most important contribution of these textiles ... was in giving us for the first time a complete set of clothes of the first and second centuries AD, worn by the Jews of Palestine, which...reflect also the fashions throughout the Roman Empire of those days"); Gildas Hamel, *Poverty and Charity in Roman Palestine* (Berkeley: University of California, 1990) 57-93 ("Poverty in Clothing"); E.P. Sanders, *Judaism: Practice and Belief 63 BCE - 66 CE* (Philadelphia: Trinity Press, 1992) 123-124. Cf. Israel Abrahams, *Jewish Life in the Middle Ages* (Philadelphia: Jewish Publication Society, 1911; frequently reprinted) 273-290 ("Costume in Law and Fashion"), esp. 280, "...it may be asserted in general that there was no distinctive Jewish dress until the law forced it upon the Jews." Cf. Mendel and Thérèse Metzger, *Jewish Life in the Middle Ages* (New York: Alpine Fine Arts Collection, 1982) 111-150 ("Costume"), esp. 138, "Contrary to what might be expected, there was no tradition of clothing peculiar to Jews" (see too p. 150). See below note 32.

[14]Tertullian, *De Corona* 4.2 (= Corpus Christianorum 1:1043-1044) writes: *apud Judaeos tam sollemne est feminis eorum velamen capitis ut inde noscantur.* (Tertullian makes the same point in *De Oratione* 22 = Corpus Christianorum 1:270). Claude Aziza correctly notes that the literary context in both the *De Corona* and the *De Oratione* suggests that Tertullian derived his "evidence" from the Hebrew Bible, not from his observation of contemporary Jewish women. Nevertheless, Aziza insists that Tertullian indeed provides reliable evidence about contemporary Jewish women. Aziza supports this contention by appeal to M. Shabbat 6:6, but that Mishnah partly confirms (Jewish women veil themselves) and partly contradicts (the headcoverings worn by Jewish women are the same as those of their gentile neighbors) what Tertullian says. See Claude Aziza, *Tertullien et le Judaisme* (Paris: Les belles lettres, 1977) 20-21. On the veiling of women in public see Ramsay MacMullen, "Women in Public in the Roman Empire," *Changes in the Roman Empire: Essays in the Ordinary* (Princeton: Princeton University Press, 1990) 162; on the veiling of Arab women, see R. de Vaux, "Sur le voile des femmes dans l'orient ancien," *Revue biblique* 44 (1935) 397-412. Jewish women in Palestine too seem to have been veiled in public, but I know of no ancient evidence that would confirm Tertullian's statement that they were distinctive because of their veils. A medieval passage of uncertain date and provenance contrasts the habits of Roman with Jewish women; see Daniel Sperber, *A Commentary on Derech Erez Zuta Chapters Five to Eight* (Tel Aviv: Bar Ilan University Press, 1990) 123. In the Roman West women seem as a rule not to have veiled themselves; hence, the Jewish women of Carthage, who probably hailed from the East, appeared distinctive because they maintained the mores of their countries of origin. W.H.C. Frend, citing the passage from Tertullian, writes that "The Jew seems even at that time [second century CE] to have been distinguished by his dress, his

On the contrary, there is much evidence that Jews, whether male or female, were not easily distinguished from gentiles.

Some examples. In the romantic and novelistic retelling of scripture attributed to the Jewish writer Artapanus, the Egyptian king Chenephres "ordered the Jews to be clothed with linen and not to wear woolen clothing. He did this so that once they were so marked, they could be harassed by him." Without such a publicly visible mark, there was no way to distinguish Jews from the rest of the population.[15] According to the novella known as 3 Maccabees, when Ptolemy Philopator ordered the Jews to be registered and marked as slaves, he wanted to have them branded with an ivy leaf, "the emblem of Dionysus"; here, too, without such a publicly visible mark, there was no way to distinguish Jews from the rest of the population.[16] In the Alexandrian riots in the time of Caligula, the mob arrested Jewish women and brought them to the theater, but by mistake seized many non-Jewish women as well – obviously, Jewish women could not be easily distinguished from non-Jewish.[17] Similarly, the Babylonian Talmud reports that R. Ada b. Ahavah once spotted a woman in the market wearing a *krabalta*, an outlandish piece of clothing not precisely identifiable but obviously inappropriate for a daughter of Israel. The good rabbi, thinking the woman to be a Jew, tore off her *krabalta*, but was chagrined to discover that the woman was a gentile (and a member of the royal family). The rabbi was fined 400 zuz.[18] At the opening of Justin Martyr's *Dialogue with Trypho the Jew*, Trypho recognizes Justin immediately as a philosopher (because he is wearing the garb of a philosopher), but Justin has to ask Trypho "who are you" and has to be told "I am called Trypho and I am a Hebrew of the circumcision." Without such a statement, Justin would not have known Trypho to be either a Jew or circumcised.

In sum, the silence of the texts indicates that Jews were not distinctive because of their clothing.[19] This silence is striking because

---

food, his dwelling in a separate quarter of the town," but this statement is much exaggerated; see Frend, *Martyrdom and Persecution in the Early Church* (New York: New York University Press, 1967) 146 with n. 53.

[15]Artapanus, frag. 3 parag. 20, in Carl Holladay, *Fragments from Hellenistic Jewish Authors* (Scholars Press 1983), 1:216-217. I am grateful to Albert Pietersma for reminding me of this passage. The passage seems to be an etiological explanation for the origin of the prohibition of wearing wool and linen together (Deut. 22:11).

[16]3 Maccabees 2:29.

[17]Philo, *Against Flaccus* 96. Contrast the passage of Tertullian cited above.

[18]B. Berakhot 20a (a reference I owe to Herb Basser). I follow the reading of the Munich manuscript.

[19]According to Y. Demai 4:6 24a, the men of Jerusalem were accustomed to wear robes in the Roman style. See the discussion of the passage by Daniel Sperber,

ancient Jewish sources describe two distinctively Jewish items of clothing: *tzitzit* and *tefillin*. Jesus, the Pharisees, and presumably other pietists in the land of Israel wore *tzitzit* in public, tasseled fringes affixed to the four corners of one's garment in accordance with the injunctions of Numbers 15:37-41 and Deuteronomy 22:12. *Tzitzit* of the period of Bar Kochba have been discovered in the Judaean desert. The Pharisees and other pietists in the land of Israel also wore *tefillin* in public, usually called "phylacteries," small leather containers strapped to the head and arm and containing several excerpts from the Torah, notably the *Shema* and (in some versions) the ten commandments. *Tefillin* have been discovered at Qumran.[20]

According to one rabbinic legend of Babylonian provenance a pious Jew working as a jailer kept his Jewishness secret by wearing black shoes (apparently Babylonian Jews did not wear black shoes) and by not wearing *tzitzit*.[21] According to another statement Jews ought not to sell to a gentile a garment fringed with *tzitzit* because, R. Judah explains, the gentile might don the garment, accost an unsuspecting Jew, and kill him.[22] Thus, in rabbinic piety, *tzitzit* could serve as a marker to distinguish Jew from gentile and, indeed, to hamper intimate relations between Jewish men and gentile women.[23] In the rabbinic imagination

---

"Melilot V," *Sinai* 91 (1982) 270-275 (Hebrew), a reference I owe to Marc Bregman. All in all it is striking to note the large number of Greek and Latin words used by the rabbis to denote items of clothing. Genesis Rabbah 82:8 p. 984 ed. Theodor is a story about two disciples who in a time of persecution "changed their dress." This story is usually understood to mean that the disciples changed their clothing so that they would not be recognized as Jews (see for example Theodor's commentary ad loc. and *Shulhan Arukh, Yoreh Deah* 157:2), but it is more likely that the story simply means that the disciples were trying to hide their status as rabbis. Normally disciples of sages (like philosophers) were immediately recognizable by their clothing (see Sifre Deuteronomy 343 p. 400 ed. Finkelstein and parallels), but these disciples tried to hide their standing as rabbis in order to escape a persecution that was directed primarily at the sages.

[20]See the evidence, references, and bibliography assembled by Emil Schürer, *The History of the Jewish People in the Age of Jesus Christ*, rev. and ed. G. Vermes, F. Millar, et al. (3 vols; Edinburgh: T. & T. Clark, 1973-1987) 2:479-481. On the *tzitzit* see Yadin, *Bar Kochba* 81-84. Following Epiphanius Goodenough argues that *phylacteria* in Matthew 23:5 means not "*tefillin*" but "stripes of purple cloth appliqué"; see Goodenough, *Jewish Symbols* 9:171-172. It is not clear whether the tassels that appear on the clothing of some of the painted figures of the Dura-Europus synagogue are *tzitzit* or merely tassels; see Carl H. Kraeling, *The Excavations at Dura-Europus: The Synagogue* (New Haven: Yale University Press, 1956; repr. New York: Ktav, 1979) 81 n. 239.

[21]B. Taanit 22a; on black shoes see B. Sanhedrin 74b (top).

[22]B. Menahot 43a (a reference I owe to Ranon Katzoff). The Talmud also supplies another explanation for the rule, but its meaning is not clear.

[23]B. Menahot 44a (and parallels).

tefillin could serve the same function.[24] The Letter of Aristeas mentions both *tzitzit* and *tefillin;* Philo and Josephus also mention the *tefillin*.[25] Greek speaking Jews in the diaspora thus knew of *tzitzit* and *tefillin,* but, unlike the rabbis, they never refer to them as markers of Jewish identity.

Why do outsiders not mention either *tzitzit* or *tefillin?* We have three possibilities: (1) Jews (like diaspora Jews) who came into contact with outsiders did not wear *tzitzit* and *tefillin* in public, and perhaps not at all; (2) Jews did wear *tzitzit* and *tefillin,* but outsiders did not find them remarkable; or (3) Jews wore *tzitzit* and *tefillin* in an inconspicuous manner so as not to attract the attention of outsiders. I think that explanation (1) is by far the most plausible. According to one rabbinic passage, togas and two other specific forms of Roman (Greek?) clothing were exempt from the commandment of *tzitzit;* Romanized Jews – who probably would not have listened to the rabbis anyway – were under no obligation to wear *tzitzit*.[26]

To summarize these first two points: Jews were not distinctive either by their looks or their clothing. Jews of Antioch looked Antiochene, Jews of Alexandria looked Alexandrian, Jews of Ephesus looked Ephesian, and the Jews of Rome looked like just another exotic group from the east.

Not a single ancient author says that Jews are distinctive because of their speech. The Jews of the diaspora in the middle ages created a number of distinctive Jewish "languages": Judaeo-Arabic, Judaeo-German (Yiddish), Judaeo-Greek, Judaeo-Spanish (Ladino), Judaeo-Persian. The Jews of antiquity, however, did not. The common language of the Jews of the Roman empire (perhaps including Palestine) was Greek. Literate Jews (like Philo) spoke a literate Greek, while illiterate Jews spoke a Greek that was the target of sneers from the educated.[27] There is no evidence at all for a "Jewish Greek," or even for Jewish slang.[28] Jews spoke Greek like everyone else.[29]

Not a single ancient author says that Jews are distinctive because of their names. The Tosefta remarks, "Writs of divorce that come (that is, that are

---

[24]Fathers according to Rabbi Nathan B 19 pp. 21a-b ed. Schechter.

[25]Aristeas 157-158; Josephus, *Jewish Antiquities* 4.213; Naomi G. Cohen, "Philo's Tefillin," *Proceedings of the World Congress for Jewish Studies* (1985). Unless I am mistaken neither Philo nor Josephus mentions *tzitzit*.

[26]Sifre Deuteronomy 234 pp. 266-267 ed. Finkelstein.

[27]Cleomedes apud Stern #333.

[28]In contrast, German Jews of the lower classes did create a distinctive Jewish German slang which even non-Jewish Germans adopted; see Werner Weinberg, *Die Reste des Jüdischdeutschen* (Stuttgart: Kohlhammer, 1969).

[29]Kurt Treu, "Die Bedeutung des griechischen für die Juden im römischen Reich," *Kairos* 15 (1973) 123-144; G.H.R. Horsley, "The Fiction of Jewish Greek," *New Documents Illustrating Early Christianity* 5 (1989) 5-40.

brought to the land of Israel) from overseas are valid, even if the names (of the witnesses) are like the names of the gentiles, because Israel(ites) overseas (have) names like the names of the gentiles."[30] Some diaspora Jews had Jewish or Hebrew names, but many, perhaps most, had names that were indistinguishable from those of the gentiles, a fact that is confirmed by the epigraphical and archaeological record. Many Jews in antiquity, in both the land of Israel and the diaspora, had two names, one gentile and the other Jewish; when they used their gentile names their Jewishness was well hidden.[31]

On the importance of distinctive Jewish names and language for the maintenance of Jewish identity in the diaspora, the rabbis comment as follows:[32]

> R. Huna said in the name of Bar Qappara,
> Because of four things were the Israelites redeemed from Egypt:
> because they did not change their names;
> and they did not change their language;
> and because they did not speak ill (of each other);
> and because none of them was sexually promiscuous.

> "Because they did not change their names":
> They went down (to Egypt) Reuben and Simeon, and they came up Reuben and Simeon.

---

[30]T. Gittin 6:4 p. 270 L (and parallels). The Yerushalmi ad loc asks how we can be sure that the witnesses are, in fact, Jews; see below.

[31]Diaspora Jews did show a fondness for certain names, or certain kinds of names, and some diaspora Jews did use Hebrew names. Still, outsiders did not comment on the peculiar names of the Jews probably because Jews who came into contact with outsiders did not have peculiar names. On names of Jews in antiquity see Juster, *Juifs* 2:221-234; Naomi G. Cohen, "Jewish Names as Cultural Indicators in Antiquity," *Journal for the Study of Judaism* 7 (1976) 97-128; Heikki Solin, "Juden und Syrer im westlichen Teil der römischen Welt," *Aufstieg and Niedergang der römischen Welt* II 29.2 (*Principat: Sprache und Literatur*) (1983) 587-789, at 636-647 and 711-713; J. Reynolds and R. Tannenbaum, *Jews and Godfearers at Aphrodisias* (Cambridge: Cambridge Philological Society, 1987) 93-105; and the recent Hebrew University dissertation by Tal Ilan.

[32]Leviticus Rabbah 32:5 pp. 747-748 ed. Margaliot and numerous parallels. In the parallel in Pesiqta de Rav Kahana Beshallah p. 83b ed. Buber (= p. 182 ed. Mandelbaum), Buber refutes a popular paraphrase of this midrash which adds the clause "because they did not change their clothing." Buber comments (n. 66), "This our sages of blessed memory never said." In all likelihood Buber is correct, although some later versions do, in fact, read "because they did not change their clothing." See the variants assembled and discussed by Menahem M. Kasher, *Torah Shelemah* 8 (5714 = 1954) 239, and 9 (5715 = 1955) 116 (I owe this reference to Herb Basser and Marc Bregman).

They did not call Reuben "Rufus," Judah "Lollianus," Joseph "Justus,"[33] and Benjamin "Alexander."

This midrash sees the sojourn of the Israelites in Egypt as prefiguring the exile/diaspora. Presumably the midrash is commenting negatively on the status quo; the Israelites of old were redeemed but we are not, because the Israelites of old merited redemption but we (that is, all Jews, not just the Jews of the diaspora) do not. We have changed our names, we have changed our language, we do speak ill of each other (*lashon hara'*), and we are sexually promiscuous (that is, certain members of our community have intermarried[34]). The Jews of both the diaspora and the land of Israel changed their names and changed their language.

Not a single ancient author says that Jews are distinctive because of their occupations. As is well known in modern western societies certain professions and trades have attracted inordinately large numbers of Jews. As is also well known, in medieval Christian Europe Jews were allowed to pursue only a limited number of occupations. In antiquity, however, Jews did not segregate themselves, and were not segregated by general society, in their occupations. The economic profile of the Jews of antiquity seems to have been identical with that of their gentile neighbors, whether in the diaspora or in the land of Israel. Jews in Rome were widely reputed to be beggars, but no ancient source suggests that all beggars were Jews or that all Jews were beggars.[35] Jews perhaps abstained from certain occupations which would have brought them into contact with the gods and religious ceremonies of the gentiles, but, as far as is known, they did not concentrate in particular professions or devote themselves to particular trades. There were no "Jewish" occupations in antiquity.[36]

Romans can pass as Jews without difficulty

Jews and gentiles in antiquity were corporeally, visually, linguistically, and socially indistinguishable. Even the sages of the

---

[33]All the manuscripts of Leviticus Rabbah read "LYSTS," that is "Lestes" (the Greek word for "brigand"), but I presume that the initial "l" is an erroneous duplication from the previous word (LYWSP), and that the name that is intended is "YSTS," that is, Justus.

[34]That this is the meaning of *parutz ba'ervah* is demonstrated by the subsequent discussion in the midrash.

[35]Yohanan Hans Lewy, "Jewish Poor in Ancient Rome," *Studies in Jewish Hellenism* (Jerusalem: Bialik Institute, 1969) 197-203 (Hebrew).

[36]Reynolds and Tannenbaum, *Jews and Godfearers at Aphrodisias* 116-123.

rabbinic academy could not discern Romans in their midst. The story is from the Sifre on Deuteronomy:[37]

> Once the (Roman) government sent two soldiers and said to them,
> Go and make yourselves Jews, and see what is the nature of their Torah.
> They went to R. Gamaliel in Usha,
> and they read Scripture, and they studied the Mishnah, midrash, laws and narratives.
> When the time came for them to leave, they (the soldiers) said to them (the school of R. Gamaliel),
> All of the Torah is fine and praiseworthy,
> except for this one matter which you say,
> An object stolen from a gentile is permitted (to be used), but (an object stolen) from a Jew is prohibited,
> but this matter we shall not report to the government.

In the two parallel versions of this story, the command to "make yourselves Jews" (*'asu 'atzmekhem yehudim*) is absent: the Roman officials come as Romans and leave as Romans.[38] They are not spies but inspectors. These versions of the story, however, present a problem: how could the sages teach Torah to gentiles? The Talmud explicitly says "Transmitting words of Torah to a gentile is prohibited" (B. Hagigah 13a) and R. Yohanan says "a gentile who studies Torah is liable to the death penalty" (B. Sanhedrin 59a). This problem, which bothered the medieval commentators,[39] also bothered the editor of the Sifre, who solved it by having the Roman officers "make themselves Jews."[40] Thus R. Gamaliel taught the Romans Torah because R. Gamaliel and his colleagues believed the Romans to be Jews.

---

[37]Sifre, Deuteronomy 344 p. 401 ed. Finkelstein.

[38]Y. Baba Qamma 4:3 4b; B. Baba Qamma 38a.

[39]See Tosafot on Baba Qamma 38a s.v. *qar'u.*

[40]A slightly different version of R. Yohanan's statement (not, of course, ascribed to R. Yohanan) appears in Sifre Deuteronomy 345 p. 402 ed. Finkelstein, just one page after our story. Thus the editor of the Sifre certainly knew, and approved of, the prohibition of teaching Torah to gentiles, and it is likely that the phrase "make yourselves Jews" is a redactional addition by the editor of the Sifre to a pre-existing story. See Steven Fraade, *From Tradition to Commentary* (Albany: State University of New York, 1991) 51-53, esp. 51 n. 129. Saul Lieberman argues that the phrase is an interpolation in the Sifre, but I (following Fraade) am not convinced. The strongest argument that the phrase is an interpolation is overlooked by Lieberman: the ending of the story should have contained a reference to the revelation of the officers' true identity: "when the time came for them to leave, they revealed themselves and said to R. Gamaliel etc." The absence of an unmasking may imply that no deception was involved. But I am still not convinced.

"Make yourselves Jews" probably means not "convert to Judaism" but "pretend to be Jews" or "disguise yourselves as Jews." It is hard to imagine Romans pretending to be Jews, entering a rabbinic academy, there to study the entire rabbinic curriculum, without once blowing their cover or revealing their true identity. Their accents, their looks, their initial ignorance of things Jewish and rabbinic (an ignorance which we may freely assume must have been quite impressive) – did none of this give them away? Apparently not. Some medieval copyists had such difficulty with this that they understood "make yourselves Jews" to mean "pretend to be converts" (or, less likely, "make yourselves converts"[41]) and substituted *gerim* for *yehudim*.[42] According to this "correction," the Romans presented themselves to R. Gamaliel as converts, and R. Gamaliel would have had no difficulty in accepting them as such.

If my analysis is correct, this story, as redacted by the editor of the Sifre, told of Roman soldiers pretending to be Jews and successfully surviving the scrutiny of R. Gamaliel and his colleagues. If you knew what to say and do, apparently it was easy to pass as a Jew.

Did circumcision make Jews distinctive?

Would not circumcision have made Jews distinct and recognizable? The question is complicated and requires extended discussion. I begin with the obvious: even if circumcision is an indication of Jewishness, it is a marker for only half of the Jewish population (in the eyes of the ancients the more important half, of course, but still, only half). How you would know a Jewish woman when you saw one, remains open.[43]

---

[41]In rabbinic Hebrew "to make a Jew" (*la'asot yehudi*), "to be made a Jew" (*lehe'asot yehudi*), and "to make oneself a Jew" (*la'asot atzmo yehudi*) are not standard locutions for "to convert to Judaism," even though Genesis 12:5 (*and the souls that they had made in Haran*) was taken to refer to the making of converts (Genesis Rabbah 39:14 pp. 378-379 ed. Theodor-Albeck and parallels). See Shaye J.D. Cohen, "Crossing the Boundary and Becoming a Jew," *Harvard Theological Review* 82 (1989) 13-33, at 29. For an exception see Tanhuma Shoftim 10 (*na'aseiti yisrael*, "I have become an Israelite") and the manuscript variants to B. Menahot 44a.

[42]I am arguing that *yehudim*, as the lectio difficilior, is the more original reading. *Gerim*, however, has more and better support than *yehudim* (see Fraade 214 n. 129).

[43]Unless her veil would give her away; see Tertullian above. Strabo, *Geography* 16.2.37, repeated at 16.4.9 and 17.2.5 (=Stern ##115, 118, 124) writes that the Jews practice circumcision on men and excision (*ektome*) on women. I do not know the origin of this statement: an ethnographic topos? Philo thinks that excision is practiced by Egyptians (*Questions on Genesis* 3.47).

In certain times and places circumcision would have functioned as a or the marker of Jewishness (or, in the language of the Theodosian Code, *nota iudaica*[44]), but not in all times and not in all places. On the Jewish side, circumcision became *the* marker of Jewish identity – at least in Palestine – in the Maccabean period. Jews are those who are circumcised, Greeks are those who are not; "apostate" Jews try to hide their circumcision through epispasm, the "stretching" or "drawing down" of the remains of the foreskin so that the penis would have the look of an uncircumcised organ. Those who joined the Maccabean state were circumcised as well. Greek historians recounting the Maccabean conquests knew the importance of circumcision to the Maccabees, but over a century had to elapse before outsiders began to associate circumcision with Judaism in the diaspora.[45] That association is documented by one Latin writer in Rome in the second half of the first century BCE (Horace) and by a string of Latin writers from the middle of the first century CE to the first quarter of the second century CE (Persius, Petronius, Martial, Suetonius, Tacitus, Juvenal).

Horace (65-8 BCE) once humorously refers to "the clipped Jews" (*curtis Iudaeis*).[46] Persius (34-62 CE) mocks the man who fears the Sabbath, "turning pale at the sabbath of the skinned" (literally, "you turn pale at the skinned sabbath," *recutitaque sabbata palles*).[47] In the Satyricon of Petronius (mid-first century CE) a group of characters is trying to figure out how to disembark from a ship without being recognized. The suggestion is made that they dye themselves with ink to appear to be Ethiopian slaves. The suggestion is rejected as inadequate; a good disguise requires more than mere skin coloring. "Circumcise us, too, so that we look like Jews (*etiam circumcide nos ut Iudaei videamur*), and bore

---

[44]Codex Theodosianus 16.8.22 (Theodosius II, 20 October 415 CE) = Amnon Lindner, *The Jews in Roman Imperial Legislation* (Detroit: Wayne State, 1987) #41.

[45]On the Maccabees see Shaye J.D. Cohen, "Religion, Ethnicity, and 'Hellenism' in the Emergence of Jewish Identity in Maccabean Palestine," *Religion and Religious Practice in the Seleucid Kingdom*, ed. Per Bilde et al. (Aarhus University Press, 1990) 204-223. Greek historians: Timagenes (Stern #81), Strabo (Stern #100, 115), and Ptolemy (Stern #146). On epispasm see Robert G. Hall, "Epispasm and the Dating of Ancient Jewish Writings," *Journal for the Study of Pseudepigrapha* 2 (1988) 71-86, and Nisan Rubin, "The Stretching of the Foreskin and the Enactment of *peri'ah*," *Zion* 54 (1989) 105-117.

[46]Horace *Satires* 1.9.69-70 = Stern #129. Latin *curtus* = Greek *kolobos*; see *Corpus Glossariorum Latinorum*, ed. Loewe-Goetz, 7:299 s.v. For *kolobos* used to describe circumcision, see Strabo, *Geographica* 16.4.9 = Stern #118.

[47]Persius *Satires* 5.184 = Stern #190. *cutis* means simply "skin" or "leather," but can mean "foreskin"; see J. N. Adams, *The Latin Sexual Vocabulary* (Baltimore: Johns Hopkins, 1982, repr. 1991) 73. Therefore *recutitus* means "with the (fore)skin removed."

our ears to imitate Arabians, and chalk our faces till Gaul takes us for her own sons."[48]   A remarkable epigram, probably but not certainly by Petronius, states that if a Jew (*Iudaeus*) does not "cut back with a knife the region of his groin" and "unloose by art the knotted head" (that is, skillfully remove the knot [=foreskin] from the head of the penis), "he shall wander from his ancestral city, cast forth from his people (*ni ... ferro succiderit inguinis oram et nisi nodatum solverit arte caput, exemptus populo patria migrabit ab urbe*)."[49] These two texts refer in the first instance to the Jews in their ethnic homeland (Judaeans, rather than Jews), but we may presume that Petronius intended the passages to have relevance to the Jews of Rome too.   In a third passage Petronius refers to a "skinned" slave (*recutitus est*); we cannot be sure that the slave was Jewish.[50] Martial (end of the first century CE) complains that Caelia, a Roman girl, bestows her favors on the men of many nations, including "skinned Jews" (*nec recutitorum fugis inguina Iudaeorum*), but not on Romans.[51] In a vicious attack on a rival in both poetry and love, Martial describes him (four times in only eight lines!) with the offensive word *verpus*. *Verpus* means "with the glans of the penis exposed," the glans being exposed either because of erection or because of circumcision.[52] This poetic rival, this *verpus*, "born in the very midst of Jerusalem" (*Solymis natus in ipsis*), buggers my slave (*pedicas puerum, verpe poeta, meum*) and has the nerve to deny it!   Martial knows that his readers know that anyone born in Jerusalem will be circumcised, hence the pun of the poem: the rival is *verpus* because he is circumcised and because he lusts for a boy.[53] Two

---

[48]Petronius *Satyricon* 102:14 = Stern #194.

[49]Petronius, frag. #37 = Stern #195. *patria* is the excellent emendation of E. Courtney, *The Poems of Petronius* (Atlanta: Scholars Press, 1991; American Classical Studies) 70. Stern accidentally omits the translation for *et nisi nodatum solverit arte caput. caput = glans penis*; see Adams, *Sexual Vocabulary* 72, and cf. Rutilius Namatianus, *De Reditu Suo* 1.388 (= Stern #542), *(gens) quae genitale caput propudiosa metit.*

[50]Petronius, *Satyricon* 68.8 (= Stern #193).

[51]Martial, *Epigrams* 7.30.5 = Stern #240. Book 7 was published in 92 CE; see J.P. Sullivan, *Martial: the Unexpected Classic* (Cambridge: Cambridge University, 1991) 39.

[52]Exposed because of erection: Catullus 47.4 (*verpus Priapus*), and cf. Martial 11.46.2 where *verpa* means erect penis. Exposed because of circumcision: Juvenal 14.104 (see below). The same ambiguity obtains in the parallel Greek words *pswlos/pswle*; see K. J. Dover, *Greek Homosexuality* (Cambridge: Harvard University, 1978, repr. 1989) 129. For an excellent discussion of these words see Adams, *Sexual Vocabulary* 12-14. See next note.

[53]Martial 11.94 = Stern #245. *verpus* often is used in connection with aggressive homosexual love; see Adams, and N.M. Kay, *Martial Book XI: A Commentary* (London: Duckworth, 1985) 258 (commentary on 11.94). On *pedicare* see Adams 123-125. Book 11 was published at the end of 96 CE; see Sullivan 46.

other epigrams may refer to Jews and circumcision, but the texts are difficult to interpret, and I relegate discussion to an appendix.[54]

For these four poets Jews are those who are circumcised, and those who are circumcised are, or look like, Jews (none of them associates circumcision with any other people). We should not exaggerate, of course; the perspective of these four poets was not universal even in Rome. Many other Latin writers of the same period in Rome mention – or even discuss at some length – Jews or Judaea but say nothing about circumcision.[55] Other natives of the "orient," in addition to Jews, may well have persisted in observing their ancestral custom in Rome. Celsus, a medical writer living in Rome in the middle of the first century CE, describes a medical procedure by which a man whose glans is bare "can cover it for the sake of a pleasing appearance (*decoris causa*)." The glans might be bare for natural reasons (that is, from birth), or "in someone who after the custom of certain nations has been circumcised" (*qui quarundam gentium more circumcisus est*). Jews are not mentioned.[56] Thus the Jews are not the only nation to practice circumcision (see further below), but in Rome in the first century the Jews became particularly and peculiarly associated with it.

The barbs of the satirists seem innocuous, but they, and the attitude they represent, paved the way for a radical decision by the Roman state: any circumcised person in the city of Rome would be assumed by the state to be a Jew, and whoever was assumed by the state to be a Jew was liable to the *fiscus Iudaicus,* the "Jewish tax" levied on Jews throughout the empire as war reparations for the revolt of 66-70 CE. Suetonius (first half of the second century CE) reports the following about the emperor Domitian:[57]

> Besides other (taxes), the Jewish tax was levied with the utmost vigor; (both) those who lived a Jewish life without registering (themselves as Jews), as well as those who concealed their origin and did not pay the tribute levied on their nation, were prosecuted as subject to the tax. I recall being present in my youth when a ninety year old man was examined by the procurator before a very crowded court to see whether he was circumcised.

---

[54]See Appendix A.

[55]Circumcision is not mentioned by Cicero, Varro, Ovid, Valerius Maximus, Seneca, Pliny the Elder, Valerius Flaccus, Silius Italicus, Quintilian, or Statius, although all of these Latin authors living in Rome have something to say about Jews or Judaea.

[56]Celsus, *De Medicina* 7.25.1. Celsus refers to an author named Iudaeus (Stern ## 150-151) but otherwise does not mention Jews anywhere in his book. *decoris causa* echoes Herodotus 2.37.2 (having a foreskin is *euprepes*).

[57]Suetonius *Domitian* 12.2 = Stern #320. I have modified the Loeb translation of Rolfe (reprinted by Stern) in order to make it more literal.

This story concerns those who say that they are not Jews but are, that is, they say they are not liable to the Jewish tax but are. Suetonius refers to two categories of people: those who "live a Jewish life" but have not declared themselves to be, or registered themselves as, Jews (*qui inprofessi Iudaicam viverent vitam*), and those who were born Jews but who mask their Jewish birth (*qui ... dissimulata origine*) so that they would not have to pay the tax imposed on their nation (*imposita genti tributa non pependissent*). Members of the first category were not born Jews but converts to Judaism or "judaizers," while members of the second category were born Jews who did not lead a Jewish life. Unfortunately Suetonius does not tell us what this ninety year old man did (or refrained from doing) so as to arouse the suspicions of the authorities, or whether the man was in fact circumcised, or what decision was rendered. Nor does Suetonius tell us whether the old man was suspected of belonging to the first category (that is, of being a convert or a judaizer) or the second (that is, of being an unobservant Jew or an apostate).[58] In either case, apparently, circumcision would have been seen as unmistakable proof of Jewishness, since it would have indicated either Jewish birth (circumcision being performed on the eighth day after birth) or Jewish life or both. In the eyes of the state, at least under Domitian (81-96 CE) and at least in Rome, if you were circumcised you were Jewish.[59] Presumably no one but Jews would continue to circumcise their sons.

Why did the Jews persist in practicing circumcision when no one, or hardly anyone, else in Rome did? The historian Tacitus, writing in the first decade of the second century CE, explains:[60]

---

[58]First category: E. Mary Smallwood, *The Jews under Roman Rule* (Leiden: Brill, 1981) 377. Second category: Martin Goodman, "Nerva, the *Fiscus Iudaicus* and Jewish Identity," *Journal of Roman Studies* 79 (1989) 40-44, at 40-41. For discussion of this passage see Margaret H. Williams, "Domitian, the Jews, and the 'Judaizers'," *Historia* 39 (1990) 196-211.

[59]We cannot be sure that this episode took place in Rome but it is possible that it did, perhaps likely. The date of the incident is c. 88-92 CE. See Stern's commentary. Nerva's coinage *fisci iudaici calumnia sublata* was issued under senatorial auspices in Rome, suggesting that Domitian's abusive exactions were practiced there. How did non-Jews who practiced circumcision fare under Domitian? Perhaps there were not many left.

[60]Tacitus *Histories* 5.5.1-2 = Stern #281. *hi ritus quoquo modo inducti antiquitate defenduntur: cetera instituta, sinistra foeda, pravitate valuere. nam pessimus quisque spretis religionibus patriis tributa et stipes illuc congerebant, unde auctae Iudaeorum res, et quia apud ipsos fides obstinata, misericordia in promptu, sed adversus omnes alios hostile odium. separati epulis, discreti cubilibus, proiectissima ad libidinem gens, alienarum concubitu abstinent; inter se nihil illicitum. circumcidere genitalia instituerunt ut diversitate noscantur. transgressi in morem eorum idem usurpant, nec quidquam prius imbuuntur quam contemnere deos, exuere patriam, parentes liberos fratres vilia habere.* See Stern's commentary ad loc. for a rich collection of parallels

> These rites (that is, frequent fasts, the Sabbath, unleavened bread), whatever their origin, can be defended by their antiquity; their other customs are sinister and abominable, and owe their persistence to their depravity: for the worst rascals among other peoples, renouncing their ancestral religions, always kept sending tribute and contributing to Jerusalem, thereby increasing the wealth of the Jews. Further, the Jews are extremely loyal toward one another, and always ready to show compassion, but toward every other people they feel only hate and enmity. They sit apart at meals and they sleep apart, and although as a nation they are prone to lust, they abstain from intercourse with foreign women; yet among themselves nothing is unlawful. They instituted circumcision of the genitalia so that they could be recognized by their difference. Those who are converted to their ways follow the same practice, and the earliest lesson they receive is to despise the gods, to disown their country, and to regard their parents, children, and brothers as of little account.

I have quoted this passage in full because its tone and general outlook are as significant as its specifics. Tacitus conceives of the Jews as a secret and sinister society, hostile to the civilized order and opposed to everything that the Romans hold sacred and dear.[61] Although, or perhaps because, they are hostile to outsiders, they attract a constant flow of converts, who increase their numbers, augment their wealth, and render them all the more dangerous. I shall return to this motif below. And how do the members of this secret society, whether natives or converts, recognize each other? Through circumcision. "They instituted circumcision of the genitalia so that they could be recognized by their difference" (*circumcidere genitalia instituerunt ut diversitate noscantur*). Tacitus' contemporary Juvenal (first quarter of the second century CE) has a similar conception of Judaism and circumcision.[62] Early Christianity, too, was widely regarded by its critics as a sinister and secret society whose members would recognize each other by a secret sign unknown to outsiders.[63] According to Tacitus, circumcision began

---

from both Jewish and non-Jewish texts (add Philostratus, Life of Apollonius 5.33 = Stern #403).

[61]For a brilliant analysis of this motif see Yohanan Hans Lewy, "Tacitus on the Antiquities of the Jews and their Manners," *Studies* 115-189, esp. 164-179 (Hebrew).

[62]Juvenal, *Satires* 14.96-106 = Stern #301. Converts allow their foreskins to be cut (*mox et praeputia ponunt*; for this sense of *ponere* see *Oxford Latin Dictionary* s.v., definition 6b) and lead only the circumcised to the desired fountain (*quaesitum ad fontem solos deducere verpos*). *verpus* here must mean "circumcised;" I see no alternative (see above).

[63]Lewy, "Tacitus," 173 n. 249, cites Caecilius in Minucius Felix, *Octavius* 2:9: Christians recognize each other by a secret sign in the body.

as a sign by which Jews would recognize each other; by Tacitus' own time it had become a sign by which outsiders would recognize Jews.

Thus in the city of Rome in the first century CE, certainly in the latter part of the century, circumcision served as a marker of Jewishness. But in the eastern parts of the empire, at least until the first century CE, circumcision cannot have served as such a marker because it was practiced by non-Jews as well as Jews. Balancing the literary tradition that associates circumcision exclusively with Judaism, a tradition exemplified by the Latin writers surveyed above,[64] is the the literary tradition that associates circumcision with Egypt and with nations influenced by Egypt, among them the Jews. Herodotus (mid fifth century BCE) says that the Colchians, Egyptians, and Ethiopians "are the only nations that have from the first practised circumcision," and that the Phoenicians and the Syrians of Palestine learned the custom from the Egyptians, while the Syrians of the river valleys of Asia Minor learned it from the Colchians.[65] That the Herodotean phrase "the Syrians of Palestine" means "the Jews of Palestine" is assumed by Diodorus of Sicily, argued by Josephus, and repeated by the philosopher Celsus in the middle of the second century CE.[66] Thus, in this literary tradition, the practice of circumcision is characteristic of the Egyptians, the Jews, and other nations as well.

How many of these nations preserved this ancestral ritual through the Hellenistic and Roman periods, is not clear. Herodotus already remarks that Phoenicians who mingle with the Greeks no longer circumcise their children.[67] But the practice did not die out. A Phoenician author of the Roman period writes that Kronos, the god of the Phoenicians, circumcised himself to atone for his castration of his father Ouranos. The intent of this statement surely is to explain the origins of the Phoenician practice of circumcision, a question that was

---

[64]The tradition first appears in Strabo, for whom circumcision is a sign not of hostility to other nations but of superstition (*deisidaimonia*). See Strabo *Geographica* 16.2.37 = Stern #115. The other Strabonian references to Jewish circumcision are in the Herodotean tradition; see Stern #118 and #124.

[65]Herodotus 2.104.2-3 = Stern #1. For a good discussion of this passage, see Alan B. Lloyd, *Herodotus Book II* (3 vols.; Leiden: Brill, 1976-1988) 2:157-159 (commentary on Herodotus 2.36.3) and 3:22-25 (commentary on 2.104.2-3). On the practice of circumcision by nations other than the Jews see Stern's commentary on Stern #1 and #511; Schürer-Vermes-Millar, *History* 1:537-540; and Jack M. Sasson, "Circumcision in the Ancient Near East," *Journal of Biblical Literature* 85 (1966) 473-476 (a reference I owe to Saul Olyan).

[66]Diodorus of Sicily 1.28.2-3 = Stern #55 and 1.55.5 = Stern #57; Josephus, *Jewish Antiquities* 8.262 and *Against Apion* 1.169-17; Celsus apud Origen, *Against Celsus* 1.22 = Stern #375 (pp. 233 and 265).

[67]Herodotus 2.104.4.

still live at the time of the author.[68] According to Philo "not only the Jews but also the Egyptians, Arabs, and Ethiopians and nearly all those who inhabit the southern regions near the torrid zone are circumcised," while "the nations which are in the northern regions...are not circumcised."[69] Josephus is probably more accurate: not the Egyptians but the Egyptian priests continued the practice of circumcision, a fact that is confirmed by papyrological documents of the second century CE.[70] Jerome (ca. 400 CE) confirms that still in his day (*usque hodie*) the Arabs practice circumcision.[71] We may assume that in the first century CE in portions of Asia Minor, Syria, Arabia, and perhaps Egypt, circumcision will not have been unusual and certainly will not have been a Jewish peculiarity. There is no certainty that Jewish circumcision looked exactly like Egyptian or Arab circumcision, but we may presume that in these regions circumcision alone was not an unmistakable marker of Jewishness.[72]

The situation will have changed markedly during the principate of Hadrian (117-137 CE). Precisely when and why the emperor Hadrian issued a general prohibition of circumcision, is debated, but that he did so is beyond dispute. In the Roman-Jewish war which erupted in the wake of this prohibition (commonly known as the war of Bar-Kokhba or Bar Kosba), circumcision was understood by both sides to be a marker of Jewishness; some Jews tried to remove it through epispasm.[73] Hadrian's successor, the emperor Antoninus Pius, issued a rescript permitting the Jews to circumcise their sons; that is, the general prohibition remained in

---

[68]Philo of Byblos apud Eusebius, *Praeparatio evangelica* 1.10.33 (= Jacoby, *FGrH* 790 F 2); see Albert Baumgarten, *The Phoenician History of Philo of Byblos* (Leiden: Brill, 1981) 222. I am grateful to Saul Olyan for reminding me of this passage.

[69]Philo, *Questions on Genesis* 3.48 (Loeb edition, supplement 1, p. 243).

[70]*Against Apion* 2.141; see Stern's commentary on Stern #1 and Colson's supplementary note to Philo, *On the Special Laws*, 1.2.

[71]Cited by Stern in his commentary on Stern #1. The Slavonic version of the *Jewish War* has one of the priests call Herod "an Arabian, uncircumcised" (H. St. J. Thackeray, *Josephus: The Jewish War* [Loeb Classical Library], vol. 3, p. 636). I do not know the origin or significance of this tradition.

[72]It is not clear exactly how much was cut or cut off in Egyptian circumcision; see Lloyd 2:158. Not all circumcisions are the same; see Rubin passim, and L. Duliére, "La seconde circoncision pratiquée entre juifs et samaritains," *L'Antiquité classique* 36 (1967) 553-565.

[73]On the Hadrianic decree see the pages of Stern and Schürer-Vermes-Millar cited above in note 65 (with bibliography); see too Peter Schäfer, *Der Bar Kokhba Aufstand* (Tübingen: Mohr (Siebeck), 1981) 38-50 and 233-235, and Alfredo M. Rabello, "Il problema della 'circumcisio' in diritto romano fino ad Antonino Pio," *Studi in onore di Arnaldo Biscardi* (2 vols.; Milan: Cisalpino-Goliardica, 1982) 2:187-214. On the rabbinic evidence for epispasm see the full discussion in Rubin.

place but the Jews were granted an exemption.[74]   Thenceforth throughout the Roman empire, even in the east, at least for the next century or so, circumcision would be a fairly secure sign of Jewishness.

The situation will have changed markedly again when the Syrian Elagabalus became emperor in 218 CE. He circumcised himself and several of his companions in honor of his Syrian god.[75] Perhaps this action indicates that circumcision had never died out completely among some portions of the Syrian population, but it certainly indicates that the Hadrianic prohibition was no longer in force.

Thus in certain times and places in antiquity, if you saw a circumcised person you could be fairly sure that he was a Jew.[76] In contemporary western culture the organ on which circumcision is practiced is generally kept hidden from the sight of other men. If this was true in antiquity as well, how often would you have had the opportunity to see the circumcision of another person? In the classical period (fifth and fourth centuries BCE) the Greeks noted that the readiness to appear naked in public was a distinctively Greek characteristic not shared by *barbaroi*.[77] In the words of some *barbaroi*, "There is no man more despicable than he who goes naked in public."[78] The Romans at first shared the barbarian aversion to public nudity,[79] but by the period of the Empire they had welded the Greek gymnasium to the Roman bath and had come to terms with nudity as a regular feature of public life. In the gymnasia and the baths the well-born would regularly be seen nude by their peers and their social inferiors; the low born, of course, routinely would have had their bodies exposed to the eyes of others, even outside the gymnasium and the bath, and this very fact was confirmation of their inferior status.[80]

---

[74]Linder, *Jews in Roman Imperial Legislation* #1. Egyptian priests too were granted an exemption; see above.

[75]Dio Cassius 80.11.1 (Loeb ed., vol. 9, pp. 456-457).

[76]The daughter of Pharaoh, when she saw Moses' circumcision, realized that the boy must be an Israelite; see B. Sotah 12b and the discussion of Louis Ginzberg, *Legends of the Jews* 5:399 n. 51. I ignore here the statistically insignificant cases of gentiles being circumcised, and Jews not being circumcised, for medical reasons. For the former see Josephus, *Against Apion* 2:143 and cf. Stern #539. For the latter see T. Shabbat 15.8 pp. 70-71 ed. Lieberman (and parallels) and cf. M. Nedarim 3:11 (reference to "the uncircumcised ones of Israel").

[77]Herodotus 1.10.3; Thucydides 1.6.5; Plato *Republic* 5.452c.

[78]Sifre Deuteronomy 320 p. 367 F (and parallels).

[79]Romans would cover their loins in public: Dionysius of Halicarnassus 7.72.2-3.

[80]Peter Brown, "Late Antiquity," in *A History of Private Life I: From Pagan Rome to Byzantium*, ed. Paul Veyne (Cambridge, MA: Belknap Press, 1987) 245-246. Tosefta Berakhot 2:14 p. 9 ed. Lieberman imagines that a field laborer might be naked or wearing only a thong; see Hamel, *Poverty and Charity*.

The degree to which Jews participated in the culture of the gymnasium is a question that I cannot address here. Clearly some Jews did participate.[81] If they experienced jibes from their uncircumcised colleagues[82] they had three choices: grin and bear (bare) it; stay home; or epispasm. Other Jews, offended by the public nudity of the gymnasium, had no interest in participating and kept themselves – and their circumcisions – home. How the Jews of the diaspora fared in the baths is not known. Certainly the rabbinic Jews of Palestine went to the baths,[83] and we may presume that diaspora Jews did so too. Here then you would have your chance to see if someone was circumcised.[84] Outside the bath, however, you would never know (unless you were dealing with a slave or another low-born person, whose naked body you would be able to see often).

A final point. Whether or not circumcision is an infallible or a usable indicator of Jewishness, there is no evidence that the Jews in antiquity ever actually used it as a means of detecting fellow Jews.[85] Here is an excerpt from a cycle of stories about Antoninus, the legendary Roman emperor who was a good friend of the Jews and a disciple of Rabbi Judah the Patriarch, known simply as Rabbi:[86]

> Antoninus said to Rabbi, will you let me eat of leviathan in the world to come?
> He (Rabbi) said to him, yes.
> He (Antoninus) said to him, from the Paschal lamb you will not let me eat, but you will let me eat of leviathan?
> He (Rabbi) said to him, what can I do for you, when concerning the Paschal lamb it is written (in Exodus 12:48) *but no uncircumcised person may eat of it.*
> When he heard this, he (Antoninus) went and was circumcised.

---

[81]H. A. Harris, *Greek Athletics and the Jews* (Cardiff: University of Wales, 1976); Paul Trebilco, *Jewish Communities in Asia Minor* (Cambridge: Cambridge University, 1991; SNTSMS 69) 176-177.

[82]The Roman poets surveyed above have a mocking tone towards circumcision. Apion too mocked (*khleuazei*) circumcision (Josephus, *Against Apion* 2.137 = Stern #176); Philo, Special Laws 1.2, reports that circumcision is widely "laughed at" (*gelatai*).

[83]M. Avodah Zarah 3:4. Even in Jewish bath-houses men would be naked in the presence of other men; see T. Berakhot 2:20 p. 10 L.

[84]In the bath one normally would be able to tell if a neighbor was circumcised; see Martial 7:82 = Stern #243 (if indeed *verpus* here means circumcised; see appendix A below).

[85]The Maccabees roamed the countryside checking to see whether babies were circumcised; later, we imagine, they roamed the countryside checking the Idumaeans and Ituraeans. Clearly these are special cases.

[86]Y. Megillah 1:12 72b = Y. Megillah 3:2 74a.

He (Antoninus) came (back) to him (and) said to him, my master,
look at my circumcision.

He (Rabbi) said to him (Antoninus), never in my life have I looked
at my own – (shall I look) at yours?

True, Rabbi Judah the Patriarch was unusually abstemious in this
matter,[87] but it is striking that there is not a single attested case in
antiquity of Jewish communal leaders checking the circumcision of a
supposed Jew.[88] Even Rabban Gamaliel and company did not check the
circumcision of the Roman spies that came to the academy (see above).
The shock that emerges from Suetonius' story quoted above might imply
that even the Romans did not regularly check circumcisions publicly, but
the Romans had the authority to do so if they needed to, but the Jews did
not. From the Jewish side circumcision was not a useful marker of
Jewishness.

Were there official lists or registers of Jews?

If, then, circumcision was neither infallible nor usable as a marker of
Jewishness, was there some other "empirical" or "objective" way by
which Jewishness could be confirmed? Or, to phrase the question more
specifically, if someone claimed to be Jewish by birth, could his or her
pedigree be checked? if someone claimed to be a convert, could this
claim somehow be verified? In sum, were genealogical registers and
records of conversions kept at the temple and/or at local community
archives and synagogues?

I cannot treat these questions here in any detail. There is abundant
and probative evidence that priests (*kohanim*) kept careful genealogical
records both before and after the destruction of the second temple, and
that they carefully checked (or were expected to check) the pedigrees of
their marriage partners. When the temple was still standing, these
records apparently were public and were maintained in the temple.[89]

---

[87]Buron Visotzky, "Three Syriac Cruxes," *Journal of Jewish Studies* 42 (1991) 167-
175, at 175.

[88]The Talmud has many stories of rabbis checking the pedigrees of Jews and
supposed Jews, but, as far as I know, no story about rabbis checking
circumcisions. In the rabbinic imagination Abraham stands at the gate to
Gehenna, refusing entry to the circumcised and allowing only the uncircumcised
(and Jews who have had sex with gentiles) to enter (B. Eruvin 19a). A gate-
keeper checking circumcision is a product of fantasy with no analogue in the real
life of rabbinic society.

[89]Saul Lieberman, *Hellenism in Jewish Palestine* (New York: Jewish Theological
Seminary, 1950) 172. On the concern of the priests to maintain family purity, see
Adolph Büchler, *Studies in Jewish History* (London: Oxford University Press, 1956)
64-98.

Whether lay Jews, too, were similarly obsessed with their genealogies, is not as clear. In any case, virtually all the evidence on the question either derives from, or refers to, the land of Israel.[90] In the Roman diaspora, certainly after 70 CE, there is no evidence for obsession with genealogical purity and hardly any evidence for public archives and archival records. A lone papyrus from Egypt refers to "the archive of the Jews" (13 BCE) in which appparently wills were filed; a lone inscription from Hierapolis in Phrygia refers to "the archive of the Jews" (the second or third centuries CE) where apparently copies of tomb violation inscriptions were recorded.[91] Public archives may have existed in various communities, then, but there is no sign that they were repositories of demographic data or were used to verify status claims. Various individuals may have kept private family genealogies, but there were no public archives that would have been of use.

A register for converts is even less likely to have existed. Julius Africanus would have us believe that in the time of Herod, "the Hebrew families, and those traceable to proselytes such as Achior the Ammonite and Ruth the Moabite, and the mixed families which had come out of Egypt" – all these were "enrolled in the archives" (*anagraptwn en tois archeiois*).[92] The plausibility of this claim is not enhanced by its reference to Achior the Ammonite, a fictional character of the book of Judith; Ruth the Moabite, a fictional (or, at least, legendary) character of the book of Ruth, the progenitrix of the royal Davidic house (and no one else), and scarcely a convert or proselyte in the later sense of the word; and the mixed multitudes who left Egypt with the Israelites, people who lived (insofar as we can say anything positive about them) approximately one thousand or twelve hundred years before the time of these archives. Furthermore, before the rabbinic innovations of the second century of our era, conversion to Judaism was entirely a private affair. The conversion was not supervised or sponsored by anyone, and there were no established standards that had to be met (except for the act itself –

---

[90]Schürer-Vermes 2:240-242, and Joachim Jeremias, *Jerusalem in the Time of Jesus* (Philadelphia: Fortress, 1969) 214-216 and 275-283. Babylonian Jews prided themselves on the purity of their pedigree (boasting that it was superior even to that of the Jews of the land of Israel – B. Qiddushin 69b and 71b), but as far as I know they never refer to a *megillat yohasin* like M. Yebamot 4:13.

[91]*Corpus Papyrorum Judaicarum* #143.7-8; *Corpus Inscriptionum Judaicarum* #775. CIJ #776 and ##778-779 (also Hierapolis) and CIJ #741 (Smyrna) refer to "the archive," but it is not clear if the reference is to "the archive of the Jews" or to the local municipal archives.

[92]Julius Africanus apud Eusebius *Historia Ecclesiastica* 1.7.13 (trans. K. Lake).

circumcision).   Conversion was entirely private and personal.[93]   A register for converts before the second or third century CE is impossible to conceive; a register for converts after the second or third century CE is conceivable but undocumented.

In sum, genealogical investigation would have been based not on documents but on the memory of oral informants.[94] This investigation will have been slow and uncertain. Without documentary records on which to rely, it is easy to see how genealogies could be forgotten, falsified, or improved. Herod the Great could try to pass himself off as a Judaean blue-blood, a descendant of the Jews who returned from Babylonia in the time of the Persians, while his opponents would call him a "half-Jew" or a "slave."[95] Paul would declare himself to be a well-bred Jew of the tribe of Benjamin, but his opponents (probably after his death) would declare him to be a gentile by birth and a convert.[96]

But even if the Jews of antiquity possessed written genealogical records, we should not exaggerate their significance or utility.   The legitimate offspring of Roman citizens were enrolled in public registers, as were all those who received grants of Roman citizenship,[97] but doubts and uncertainties were not unusual. According to Suetonius the emperor Claudius prohibited noncitizens from adopting Roman nomenclature and passing themselves off as citizens.[98] Three Alpine tribes thought that they had been granted Roman citizenship and were dismayed to discover that they had not; Claudius retroactively gave them

---

[93]Shaye J.D. Cohen, "The Rabbinic Conversion Ceremony," *Journal of Jewish Studies* 41 (1990) 177-203, esp. 193-196.

[94]Cf. B. Ketuvot 28b and Y. Ketuvot 2:10 26d (and parallels) regarding the *qetzitzah* ceremony. Memory, not documents, as a rule forms the basis of proof for the Attic orators as well.

[95]Nicolaus of Damascus apud Josephus, *Jewish Antiquities* 14.9 = Stern #90; see Stern's commentary ad loc.

[96]Epiphanius, *Panarion* 30.16.8-9 (citing the Ebionite *Ascents of James*). This motif is absent from Gerd Luedemannn, *Opposition to Paul in Jewish Christianity* (Minneapolis: Fortress, 1989), which treats material up to about 200 CE; in all likelihood the motif is a polemical invention from the third or fourth century.

[97]Registration of offspring: A. N. Sherwin-White, *Roman Society and Roman Law in the New Testament* (Oxford: Clarendon, 1963) 146-149; *Fontes Iuris Romani Antejustiniani* III ##1-5; *Historia Augusta,* Marcus Aurelius 9.7-8. Registration of citizenship grants: *Fontes Iuris Romani Antejustiniani* III ##6-8. In general see Carroll A. Nelson, *Status Declarations in Roman Egypt* (Amsterdam: A.M. Hakkert, 1979); Jane Gardner, "Proofs of Status in the Roman World," *Bulletin of the Institute of Classical Studies (London)* 33 (1986) 1ff; *New Documents Illustrating Early Christianity* 6 (1992) section 17.

[98]S. Claudius 25 *peregrinae condicionis homines vetuit usurpare Romana nomina dumtaxat gentilicia. civitatem romanam usurpantes in campo esquilino securi percussit.*

citizenship.[99] One hundred years later, the rule book of the chief finance officer of the province of Egypt threatens punishment for those who style themselves incorrectly, that is, who adopt Roman names although they are not citizens. It also threatens punishment for those Egyptians who after the death of their father declare (falsely) that their father had been a Roman citizen.[100] The jurists deal with the status problems that arise from cases of marriage in which one partner is misinformed about the status of the other.[101]

If you knew what to do and say, it must have been easy to pass as a Roman citizen, public registers or no public registers. If a person in antiquity claimed to be a Roman citizen apparently he was believed without investigation. In Acts' story of Paul's arrest and trial, Paul merely has to declare that he is a Roman citizen and he is immediately believed; he produces no documentation and is never asked to prove his status. There must have been many people who said they were Romans but were not.[102] And there may well have been many people who said they were Jews but were not.

Social mechanisms which made (or might have made) Jews distinctive

If, then, circumcision was neither an infallible or a usable marker of Jewishness; if there were no genealogical records that would have proven who was a Jew and who was not; and if the Jews of antiquity looked like everyone else, spoke like everyone else, were named liked everyone else, and supported themselves like everyone else, how did you know a Jew in antiquity when you saw one? There were two methods by which you might have established certain plausibilities or probabilities. You might reasonably conclude that people you see associating with Jews are themselves Jews, and you might reasonably conclude that people you see observing Jewish laws are Jews. These conclusions would be plausible or probable, to be sure, but not probative, as I shall now explain.

---

[99]*Fontes Iuris Romani Antejustiniani* I #71 = E. M. Smallwood, *Documents Illustrating the Principates of Gaius Claudius and Nero* (Cambridge: Cambridge University, 1967) #368.

[100]Gnomon of the Idios Logos 42-43. Cf. the Ptolemaic prohibition of changing one's name or ethnic origin: Joseph Mélèze Modrzejewski, "Le statut des Hellènes dans l'Égypte lagide," *Revue des études grecques* 96 (1983) 241-268, at 244.

[101]Gaius, *Institutes* 1.67-75, 87; 2.142-143; Ulpian 7.4; Gnomon of the Idios Logos 39, 46, 47.

[102]Perhaps Paul was one of them; see the cautious doubts of Wolfgang Stegemann, "War der Apostel Paulus ein römischer Bürger?" *Zeitschrift für das neutestamentliche Wissenschaft* 78 (1987) 200-229 and the discussion in *New Documents Illustrating Early Christianity* 6 (1992) section 20.

Jewish by association

You might reasonably conclude that people you see associating with Jews are themselves Jews. This argument has some merit especially if the Jews of antiquity as a rule kept themselves separate from gentiles. Many anti-Jewish writers refer to Jewish misanthropy (hatred of the rest of the humanity) and separateness, analogues to the charge of "clannishness" that would be advanced against Jews in modern times. In the passage cited above Tacitus says of the Jews that "toward every other people they feel only hate and enmity. They sit apart at meals and they sleep apart, and although as a nation they are prone to lust, they abstain from intercourse with foreign women." "Those who are converted to their ways," Tacitus continues, are taught "to despise the gods, to disown their country, and to regard their parents, children, and brothers as of little account." Many other sources, too, speak of the separation of Jews from gentiles, especially at table. In the book of Acts Peter tells the Roman centurion, "you yourselves know how unlawful it is (*hws athemiton estin*) for a Jew to associate with (*kollasthai*) or to visit (*proserchesthai*) anyone of another nation" (Acts 10:28). If in fact diaspora Jews separated themselves rigorously from their gentile neighbors, you could reasonably assume that people you see associating with Jews are themselves Jews.

We may be sure that many, if not most, diaspora Jews observed the Jewish food laws at least to some degree, abstaining from pork, blood, and meat "sacrificed to idols," and that these observances were a barrier to free social intercourse between Jews and gentiles, but we may not conclude that many or most diaspora Jews sought complete separation from their gentile environment. On the contrary. The bulk of the evidence suggests that the musings of the anti-Jewish writers are highly exaggerated and that diaspora Jews maintained their Jewish identity even as they integrated themselves into gentile society.[103] Even Tacitus – Juvenal, too – admits that the Jews attracted converts, a fact that clearly implies that the Jews did not separate themselves totally from their neighbors and that the boundary between Jews and gentiles was crossable. Clearly this is not the place for a full discussion of this

---

[103]Food laws: E.P. Sanders, *Jewish Law from Jesus to the Mishnah* (London: SCM, 1990) 272-283. Maintenance of Jewish identity and integration into gentile society: see the essays of A. T. Kraabel, now conveniently collected in *Diaspora Jews and Judaism: Essays in Honor of, and in Dialogue with, A. Thomas Kraabel*, ed. J. Andrew Overman and Robert S. MacLennan (Atlanta: Scholars Press, 1992); Trebilco, *Asia Minor* passim, esp. 173-183; Tessa Rajak, "Jews and Christians as Groups in a Pagan World," *"To See Ourselves as Others See Us"*, 247-262.

question which has already generated a substantial bibliography; the evidence is abundant and unequivocal.[104]

A widely quoted rabbinic passage shows that diaspora Jews did not follow an ethic of separation from gentiles. The Tosefta comments:[105]

> R. Simeon b. Eleazar says,
> Israel(ites) in the diaspora are worshippers of idolatry.[106]
> How?
> A gentile makes a (wedding) feast for his son and goes and invites all the Jews who dwell in his city –
> even though they (the Jews) eat and drink from their own, and their own steward stands and serves them,
> (nevertheless) they are worshippers of idolatry,
> as it is written *(You must not make a convenant with the inhabitants of the land, for they will lust after their gods and sacrifice to their gods) and invite you and you will eat of their sacrifices* (Exodus 34:15).

According to R. Simeon b. Eleazar, even if diaspora Jews observe the laws of kashruth, avoiding prohibited foods and foods cooked by gentiles, nevertheless their diaspora setting will inevitably bring them into intimate social contact with gentiles and thereby to social settings (like wedding feasts) which feature idolatry.[107] R. Simeon b. Eleazar, of course, is right. Diaspora Jews, even when maintaining their identity, did (and do!) routinely find themselves in intimate contact with gentiles.

Contact with gentiles took place even in the institutional life of the Jewish community. Gentiles participated in the annual festival, celebrated by the Alexandrian Jewish community, commemorating the completion of the Septuagint.[108] The pilgrimage festivals at the temple in Jerusalem attracted not only large numbers of Jews from the diaspora but also large numbers of gentiles who came to watch the proceedings.[109] The synagogues of the Roman diaspora were open to gentiles, and some

---

[104]See the massive new study *Jews and Gentiles in the Ancient World* by Louis H. Feldman (forthcoming). The frequency of intermarriage between Jews and non-Jews in antiquity is unknown.

[105]Tosefta Avoda Zara 4(5).6 p. 466 Z. For discussion of the manuscript variants and parallels, see Zvi Aryeh Steinfeld, "On the Prohibition of Eating with a Gentile," *Sidra: A Journal for the Study of Rabbinic Literature* 5 pp. 131-148 (Hebrew).

[106]Some manuscripts and testimonia read "worshippers of idolatry in purity."

[107]Cf. Canon 7 of the Council of Ancyra (314 CE) (ed. Mansi, vol. 2, p. 516): Christians who have attended pagan feasts require penance, even if they brought and ate their own food. This text was first brought to my attention by my student Ms. Susan Holman, although I now see that it was cited too by Rajak 255 n. 19 (following Baer).

[108]Philo, *Life of Moses* 2.41.

[109]Josephus *Jewish War* 6.427; cf. John 12:20. Cf. too Menander Rhetor in Stern #446. See below.

(many?) gentiles actually attended services. This was true for Asia Minor in the first century (if we may trust the book of Acts), and for Antioch and Syria in the fourth.[110] The Jewish community of Aphrodisias (in western Asia Minor) established a charitable organization which was administered (?) by a small group of Jews and proselytes, and supported (?) in part by a large number of gentiles titled "venerators of God" (*theosebeis*). These "venerators of God" probably had no formal standing in the community (any more than "righteous gentiles," gentiles who are honored by the state of Israel for saving Jews during the Holocaust, have any formal standing either in the Jewish community or the state of Israel), but they were recognized by the community for their assistance and clearly were on good terms with the Jews of the city.[111]

There is one further aspect of Jewish separatism that needs to be considered. In antiquity diaspora Jews tended to live in Jewish neighborhoods. These were not "ghettos," of course, but "ethnic neighborhoods"; members of ethnic minorities tended (and still tend!) to live in proximity to each other because they were comfortable in each other's presence and felt that their interests were better protected if they were massed as a group.[112]

In Rome the trans-Tiberian region now called Trastevere was an ethnic neighborhood with many Jews.[113] In Alexandria, Josephus says, the successors to Alexander the Great set aside for the Jews "their own district, so that they could live a life of greater purity by mixing less with strangers"; Philo reports that "the city [of Alexandria] has five sections named after the first letters of the alphabet; two of these are called `Jewish' (*Ioudaikai legontai*) because most of the Jews inhabit them (or: because most of the inhabitants are Jews), though in the rest also there

---

[110]Asia Minor: Acts 13 and 17:17; Antioch and Syria: Robert Wilken, *John Chrysostom and the Jews* (Berkeley: University of California, 1983) 66-94 ("The Attraction of Judaism"); *Apostolic Constitutions* 8.47.65 and 8.47.71. Cf. Martyrdom of Pionius 13, "I understand also that the Jews have been inviting some of you to their synagogues" (H. A. Musurillo, *The Acts of the Christian Martyrs* [Oxford: Clarendon, 1972] pp. 152-153). An inscription from Panticapaeum also seems to suggest that "God-Fearers" had a place in the synagogue of the community; see Reynolds and Tannenbaum, 54.

[111]Reynolds and Tannenbaum, *Jews and Godfearers*.

[112]The Jews of course are hardly unique in this respect. See *Corpus Papyrorum Judaicarum* vol. 1, p. 5 n. 14. Not a single non-Jewish author, not even Tacitus, comments on the fact that Jews tended to live together in Jewish neighborhoods - the phenomenon apparently was not distinctive.

[113]Philo, *Embassy to Gaius* 23.155; see the commentary of E. Mary Smallwood (Leiden: Brill, 1970) 234 ad loc., and Harry J. Leon, *The Jews of Ancient Rome* (Philadelphia: Jewish Publication Society, 1960) 135-139. On the Trastevere region see the essay by Ramsay MacMullen in this volume.

are not a few Jews scattered about."[114] Smaller settlements, too, had Jewish neighborhoods; Oxyrhynchos had a street or district called "Jewish" (*Ioudaike*), as did Hermoupolis.[115] The Jews (some Jews?) of Acmonia (in Phrygia) may have lived (if an inscription has been rightly interpreted) in "the neighborhood of those of the First-Gate."[116]

How Jewish were these "Jewish neighborhoods"?

Neighborhoods that merited the name *Ioudaike* may have been exclusively Jewish,[117] but there is no evidence that Jews had the legal or social power to exclude gentiles from their streets. In fact, the two papyrological references to the Jewish district in Oxyrhynchos describe land purchases in the district by non-Jews! At least here the name *Ioudaike* seems to have been given after the Jews no longer lived there – it was the street or neighborhood where Jews formerly had lived. In any case, only few *Ioudaikai* are known; in most cities Jewish neighborhoods will not have been exclusively Jewish. The Trastevere region of ancient Rome was home to many ethnic groups, not just Jews. And in some locations there may well have been no "Jewish neighborhood" at all; perhaps most of the Jews of these places lived in close proximity to each other, but their street or district did not attain a Jewish character.[118] It is striking that not one of the archaeologically attested synagogues from the Roman diaspora was situated in an archaeologically identifiable "Jewish neighborhood."[119]

One passage of the Yerushalmi (the Palestinian Talmud) may imply that presence in a Jewish neighborhood is sufficient to establish a presumption of Jewishness. The Yerushalmi asks: since the Jews of the diaspora use gentile names (see above), how can we ascertain the

---

[114]Josephus, *Jewish War* 2.488; Philo, *Against Flaccus* 8.55; further references and discussion in Schürer-Vermes-Millar, 3:43-44.

[115]*Corpus Papyrorum Judaicarum* #454 and #468; cf. #423. Modern scholars have deduced that Apollinopolis Magna (Edfu) too had a Jewish quarter, but there is no explicit ancient reference; see *Corpus Papyrorum Judaicarum* vol. 2 pp. 108-109.

[116]Trebilco, *Asia Minor* 78-80 with n. 101.

[117]But note the ambiguity in the Philonic passage just quoted.

[118]"Antioch had no special Jewish quarter as had Alexandria," writes David Flusser, *Encyclopedia Judaica* 3:71, s.v. Antioch. The same conclusion emerges from Carl H. Kraeling, "The Jewish Community of Antioch," *Journal of Biblical Literature* 51 (1932) 130-160, at 140-145.

[119]For the archaeological evidence see the recent survey by L. Michael White, *Building God's House in the Roman World* (Baltimore; Johns Hopkins, 1990) 60-101 ("Synagogues in the Graeco-Roman Diaspora").

Jewishness of gentile-named witnesses on writs of divorce that are sent from the diaspora to the land of Israel?[120]

> R. Bibi says in the name of R. Asi,
> (we know that the witnesses are Jewish) only if he (the scribe[121]) writes as the place (of origin of the divorce) "in the *Ioudaike*."[122]
> If there is no *Ioudaike*, (he should write) "in the synagogue."
> If there is no synagogue, he should gather together ten (Jewish) people (and write the divorce in their presence).

If a divorce was written in a *Ioudaike*, or a synagogue, or before ten (male) Jews, the Yerushalmi says that we may presume that the witnesses are Jews, even if they have gentile names. The meaning of *Ioudaike* is not certain; it may mean "Jewish district," the same meaning it has in Philo's description of Alexandria and the papyrological documents emanating from Oxyrhynchos and Hermoupolis.[123] If so, the Yerushalmi is saying that even gentile-named people in a Jewish district can presumed to be Jews. This presumption is not compelling, as I have just tried to explain. It is possible, however, that *Ioudaike* in the Yerushalmi means not "Jewish district" but "Jewish court," or some other communal Jewish institution.[124] If this is correct, the Yerushalmi is saying that even gentile-named people who appear in a document issued by a communal Jewish institution can presumed to be Jews. This presumption makes a great deal of sense. Only Jews will have submitted themselves to the authority of communal Jewish courts.[125]

In sum: people associating with Jews were not necessarily Jews themselves. Even people assembled in a synagogue or present in a Jewish neighborhood were not necessarily Jews themselves. In the Roman diaspora social mingling between Jews and gentiles was such that, without inquiring or checking, you could not be sure who was a Jew and who was not.

---

[120]Y. Gittin 1:1 43b.

[121]Or, if not the scribe, the messenger who is bringing the divorce from abroad.

[122]Alternative translation: writes (as the place of origin of the divorce) "in the place of the *Ioudaike*."

[123]See Saul Lieberman, *Studies in Palestinian Talmudic Literature*, ed. David Rosenthal (Jerusalem: Magnes, 1991) 475-476 (Hebrew), and *Tosefta K'Fshuta* on *Gittin* pp. 790-791.

[124]See Lieberman.

[125]The nature and authority of these courts – indeed, their very existence – are not my concern here.

Jewish by observance

You might reasonably conclude that people you see observing Jewish laws are Jews. The Romans understood that the observance of Jewish laws was an essential aspect of Jewishness. Thus in 49/8 BCE the proconsul L. Lentulus granted special privileges to Roman citizens in Ephesus who were Jews, and defined the category "Jews" to mean "those who have and observe Jewish sacred things," or "whoever seem to me to have and observe Jewish sacred things." I am not sure exactly what these phrases mean, but it is clear that if someone wanted to be treated as a Jew by the state he had to behave as a Jew, that is, observe Jewish laws.[126] According to Dio Cassius, a historian of the early third century CE, "from that time forth [that is, after 70 CE] it was ordered that the Jews who continued to observe their ancestral customs should pay an annual tribute of two *denarii* to Jupiter Capitolinus."[127] Only Jews who observed the ancestral customs were, at least at first, subject to the tax; it was the wicked Domitian who tried to extend the tax even to those who did not observe the laws (see above).

Thus the Jewishness of Jews expressed itself primarily, at least in the eyes of outsiders, via the observance of Jewish practices. This fact is confirmed by the word *ioudaizein,* "to judaize." Ancient Greek has many verbs that are compounds of the name of a region or ethnic group with the stem *-izein.* These verbs have three basic meanings: (a) to give political support (for example, *medizein,* perhaps the oldest and best known of these verbs, means to give political support to the Medes or Persians, that is, to side with the Medes); (b) to adopt customs or manners (for example, *phoinikizein* means to adopt the customs and manners of the Phoenicians, in this case, "unnatural vice"; *sikelizein* means to adopt the manners of the Sicilians, that is, to dance in a particular manner or play the rogue; and (c) to speak a language (for example, *surizein* means to speak Syrian; *illurizein* means to speak Illyrian). Some verbs have a combination of these meanings. Aside from a small number of passages in which *ioudaizein* might mean to give political support to the Jews (a), the verb always means to adopt the customs and manners of the Jews (b), and the customs and manners that are intended are not moral but religious. "To judaize" in antiquity does not mean to dance in a peculiar manner, or to dress in a peculiar manner, or to speak quickly, or to gesticulate with the hands while speaking; nor

---

[126]Josephus, *Jewish Antiquities* 14.228 and 234; cf. too 14.237 (the clause *an autwi phane* is parallel to *moi...edokoun* in 234; correct accordingly Marcus' translation in the Loeb) and 240. On these laws see Christiane Saulnier, "Lois romaines sur les juifs," *Revue biblique* 88 (1981) 161-198 at 168-169.
[127]Dio Cassius 66.7.2 = Stern #430.

does it mean to lend money at interest, a meaning it will have in the middle ages; rather it means to abstain from pork, to refrain from work on the Sabbath, or to attend synagogue. What makes Jews distinctive, and consequently what makes "judaizers" distinctive, is the observance of the ancestral laws of the Jews.[128]

Therefore if you see someone observing Jewish rituals, you might reasonably conclude that the person is Jewish.[129] The Tanhuma, a medieval midrash of uncertain date, tells the following story.[130] Astrologers predicted that two people seen leaving the city of Tiberias would not return home because they would be bitten by a snake and die. When they returned home safely the astrologers asked them "what did you do today"? They replied, "we did nothing today except for what we are accustomed to do: we recited the *shema* and we prayed (the Eighteen Benedictions)." The astrologers replied to them, "you are Jews? the words of astrologers have no effect on you, because you are Jews." In this story the astrologers had no idea that the people were Jewish; they did not recognize them by their clothing, gait, speech, or even by the fact that they were seen leaving the city of Tiberias, a city that was (almost) exclusively Jewish. The astrologers realized that the men were Jews only when they heard that they recited the *shema*. Recitation of the *shema* is presumptive proof of Jewishness.[131]

But is practice of Jewish laws inevitably proof of Jewishness? Dio Cassius writes that "[the citizens of the country] have been named Jews (*Ioudaioi*). I do not know how this title came to be given them, but it applies also to all the rest of mankind, although of alien race, who are

---

[128]Shaye J.D. Cohen, "The Meanings of *ioudaizein*," (forthcoming); on *ioudaizein* and its derivatives in European languages in the Middle Ages and Renaissance, see Róbert Dán, "'Judaizare' – The Career of a Term," in *Antitrinitarianism in the Second Half of the Sixteenth Century*, ed. R. Dán and A. Pirnát (Budapest: Hungarian Academy of Sciences, 1982) 25-34.

[129]And if you see someone not observing Jewish rituals, you might reasonably conclude that the person is not Jewish. Cf. Tanhuma Balaq 24 ed. Buber (and numerous parallels): a restauranteur sees that a customer neither washes his hands nor recites a benediction before eating, and deduces (incorrectly, it turns out) that the customer is a gentile. The aphorism on which the story depends is in B. Hullin 106a and Yoma 83b. I am grateful to Herb Basser for reminding me of this story.

[130]Tanhuma (nidpas) Shoftim 10 p. 114a. I thank Ranon Katzoff for bringing this text to my attention and pointing out how it differs from its parallels (see next note).

[131]It is striking that the Tanhuma shifts the burden of the story from the protective power of good deeds (like reciting the *shema*, giving charity, respecting one's neighbor), the point of the parallels in Y. Shabbat 6:10 8d and B. Shabbat 156b, to the protective power of Jewishness.

devoted to their customs."[132]   Dio is not necessarily talking about "converts" – he does not even mention circumcision. For Dio anyone devoted to Jewish ways is called a Jew.

Anyone who has read Plato knows the critical difference between "being" and "being called," between "name" and "nature." According to Dio if you are devoted to Jewish ways you are called a Jew, but are you a Jew? Some ancient texts clearly make the distinction between "being" a Jew and being "called" a Jew.[133]   Ptolemy, an otherwise unknown biographer of Herod the Great, writes that Jews and Idumaeans differ in that Jews "are so originally and naturally" (*hoi ex arches phusikoi*) while Idumaeans were called Jews only when they were conquered by the Jews and compelled to follow Jewish laws.[134]   Revelation, in the passages treated at the beginning of this study, speaks of people who call themselves Jews but really are not. A contemporary of John of Patmos, the philosopher Epictetus, writes:[135]

> Why, then, do you call yourself a Stoic [if you are a student of Epicurus], why do you deceive the multitude, why do you act the part of a Jew when you are Greek? Do you not see in what sense men are severally called Jew, Syrian, or Egyptian? For example, whenever we see a man facing two ways at once,[136] we are in the habit of saying, "He is not a Jew, he is only acting the part." But when he adopts the attitude of mind of the man who has been baptized and has made his choice, then he both is a Jew in fact and is also called one (*tote kai esti twi onti kai kaleitai Ioudaios*). So we also are counterfeit "Baptists," ostensibly Jews, but in reality something else (*houtws kai hemeis parabaptistai logwi men ioudaioi ergwi d'allo ti*).

---

[132]Dio Cassius 37.17.1 = Stern #406.

[133]Cf. Ignatius, *Letter to the Magnesians* 4, "It is proper not only to be called Christians but (also) to be (Christians)." This distinction might also be attested in a Miletus theater inscription whose exact interpretation has been disputed. If it means "For those Jews who are also known as Venerators of God," the inscription is referring to gentiles who are known as Jews because of their veneration of the god of the Jews. But this interpretation of the inscription is only one of several possibilities; see Reynolds and Tannenbaum 54.

[134]Ammonius, *De adfinium vocabulorum differentia* #243 = Stern #146. Cf. Ammonius #231, which distinguishes Thebans, the original settlers of Boeotia, from Thebageneis, later settlers who were added to the Boeotians by the Thebans, and #252, which distinguishes Italians, the original (*hoi archethen*) settlers of the land, from Italiotai, Greek settlers who came later.

[135]Arrian, *Dissertations of Epictetus* 2.19-21 = Stern #254.

[136]Oldfather in the Loeb, followed by Stern, translates "halting between two faiths," but this translation is too theological. My translation is based on Epictetus' use of the same word (*epamphoterizein*) in 4.2.4-5 (a passage similar to this one).

Whether Epictetus has Christian Jews or regular Jews in mind here, does not much matter for my purposes. Epictetus is interested in the correct application of names, and knows of people who act the part of Jews, are called Jews, but are not Jews. They become Jews only when they have made their choice and have been baptized; before that, they are prevaricators. Unfortunately Epictetus does not describe how one "acts the part of a Jew." Presumably one does so by observing one or another of the Jewish laws. In his life of Cicero, Plutarch, another contemporary of John of Patmos, reports an anecdote according to which the orator asked a suspected "judaizer" why he, "a Jew," involved himself in a case featuring a *verres* (a pig).[137] For Plutarch a "judaizer" who abstains from pork can be called a Jew.

Even rabbinic literature is aware that non-Jews can be called Jews under certain circumstances. "Anyone who denies idolatry acknowledges the entire Torah" is a widely repeated rabbinic statement. One version of it reads "Anyone who denies idolatry is called a Jew."[138]

Thus all those who observed Jewish laws (or who "deny idolatry," whatever that means exactly[139]) could be called Jews and could be known as Jews, even if they were not Jews and even if they did not necessarily see themselves as Jews. Seneca the Elder reports that in his youth certain foreign rites were expelled from the city of Rome; Seneca is probably referring to Tiberius' expulsion in 19 CE of both the Jews and the adherents of the Egyptian god Isis. Abstention from certain animal foods, Seneca continues, was sufficient to establish a presumption of guilt, that is, a presumption of being an adherent of one of the proscribed rites. As a result Seneca, on the advice of his father, abandoned his vegetarianism.[140] A vegetarian could easily be regarded as a Jew and be punished accordingly.

There is abundant evidence that some (many?) gentiles (whether pagan or Christian) in the first centuries of our era attended Jewish synagogues (see above), abstained from work on the sabbath, and perhaps observed other Jewish rituals as well. These gentiles are often called "God-Fearers" by modern scholars, but the debate about the precise meaning and application of this term ought not to obscure the fact that such gentiles existed. If so, not everyone you saw observing a

---

[137]Stern #263.

[138]*kol hakofer ba'avodah zarah niqra yehudi*, B. Megillah 13a. Cf. Y. Nedarim 3:4 38a and B. Nedarim 25a (and parallels); Sifre Numbers 111 p. 116 ed. Horovitz; Sifre Deuteronomy 54 p. 122 ed. Finkelstein; cf. Mekilta Shirah 8 on Exodus 15:11, p. 142 ed. Horovitz-Rabin.

[139]See Bel and the Dragon 28, "The king has become a Jew". See Cohen, "Crossing the Boundary," 23.

[140]Seneca, *Epistulae Morales* 108.22 = Stern #189.

Jewish ritual would necessarily have been a Jew. Even people who, on account of their observance of Jewish laws, were widely regarded as Jews and called Jews, were not necessarily Jews and did not necessarily see themselves as Jews. The observance of Jewish laws was perhaps a somewhat more reliable indicator of Jewishness than presence in a Jewish neighborhood or association with known Jews, but it was hardly infallible.[141]

A story from the Babylonian Talmud

The fallibility of observance as an indicator of Jewishness is well illustrated by a rabbinic story from the Babylonian Talmud:[142]

> There was a gentile[143] who went up to Jerusalem and ate the Paschal sacrifices.
>
> (When he returned home) he said, it is written (in the Torah) *No foreigner shall eat of it* (Exodus 12:43), *no uncircumcised person may eat of it* (Exodus 12:48), but I, I have eaten of the very best (of it)!
>
> R. Judah b. Beteira said to him,[144] did they give you a piece of the fat-tail?
>
> He said to him, no.
>
> (R. Judah replied, in that case you did not really get the best of it.) When you go up there (next time), say to them, give me a piece of the fat-tail.
>
> When he went up (to Jerusalem), he said to them, give me a piece of the fat-tail.

---

[141] Although some gentiles donated money to Jewish institutions, perhaps those rituals which would have demanded an expenditure of money will have been the clearest indicators of Jewishness. Perhaps the best statement of Jewishness for a diaspora Jew in the pre-70 CE period was the (annual?) payment of two drachmas to the Jerusalem temple. Outsiders noticed the large amounts of money that were raised by this self-imposed Jewish "tax." Converts to Judaism would pay as well as natives (see Tacitus, cited above), but we may presume that non-converts did not. If you contributed your two-drachmas to the temple, you were declaring yourself to be a Jew, and you were declaring your desire to be seen as a Jew. Contrast the social dynamic of the *fiscus Iudaicus,* briefly discussed above: if you were obligated to pay the fiscus Iudaicus, you were seen by the Roman state as a Jew, whether or not you saw yourself as one. Sara Mandell misses the point entirely; see her "Who Paid the Temple Tax when the Jews were under Roman Rule?" *Harvard Theological Review* 77 (1984) 223-232.

[142] B. Pesahim 3b. For manuscript variants, see *Gemara Shelemah: Pesahim,* ed. Barukh Naeh and Menahem M. Kasher (Jerusalem: Torah Shelemah Institute, 1960).

[143] The vulgate printed text reads "Aramaean," but all the manuscripts read "gentile."

[144] The manuscripts provide various interpolations to explain how the gentile's comment became known to R. Judah.

They said to him, (That is impossible!) The fat-tail ascends to heaven (that is, the fat-tail is consumed completely on the altar).

They said to him, who said to you (to speak) thus?

He said to them, R. Judah b. Beteira.

They said (to themselves), what is this before us? (Why would R. Judah have suggested to this man that he make such a request?)

They investigated him and they found that he was a gentile and they killed him.

They sent (a message) to R. Judah b. Beteira, peace to you, R. Judah b. Beteira, for you are in Nisibis but your net is cast in Jerusalem.

The likelihood that this story is historical, that is, that it is describing actual events in a manner more or less resembling the way they took place, is remote.[145] The story seems to assume that the Paschal sacrifice was slaughtered and roasted by the priests who would dispense portions of meat to the populace, as if the Paschal sacrifice were like a regular peace-offering (*shelamim*). But the Paschal sacrifice was unique; it was permitted to be, and apparently often was, slaughtered by the laity, and the meat would be roasted not on the altar by the priests but on the temple mount by the lay participants themselves.[146] Further difficulties: wouldn't this gentile have wondered that R. Judah b. Beteira was assisting him to trick the priests?[147] Why did not R. Judah b. Beteira go himself to Jerusalem to bring a Paschal sacrifice and there tell the priests of this miscreant?[148] At least, why did he not send a message via someone else?[149] The anecdote is story and folktale, not history, and we are not to ask such questions of stories and folktales. Fictional or not, sensible or not, the story has an important point. The story demonstrates the superiority of the disciples of Moses to the sons of Aaron. Without

---

[145]The only point in the story that is confirmed elsewhere is the association of R. Judah ben Beteira with Nisibis. See Jacob Neusner, *History of the Jews in Babylonia I: The Parthian Period* (Leiden: Brill, 1969; second edition) 46-52.

[146]The Paschal lamb was slaughtered in the temple court (the *azarah*, M. Pesahim 5:5-7), to which a gentile was prohibited access, but the actual roasting took place either on the temple mount (*har habayit*, M. Pesahim 5:10) or in all Jerusalem (not stated explicitly in the Mishnah, but cf. M. Pesahim 7:9 and 7:12 with Albeck's note), and the eating took place anywhere in Jerusalem, to which gentiles were permitted access (M. Kelim 1:8). Cf. Schürer-Vermes 2:252 n. 55 and Sanders, *Judaism* 136-137.

[147]To avoid this difficulty see the ingenious interpretation of R. Solomon Luria (the Maharshal), followed by the Maharsha, ad loc.

[148]See Tosafot s.v. *me'alyah*.

[149]Probably because the storyteller wants to employ the dramatic but common motif of the deceived messenger who brings a message that will lead to his own death. See Stith Thompson, *Motif Index of Folk Literature* (6 vols; Bloomington: Indiana University, 1932-1936) motif K978, the "Uriah letter motif."

the assistance of R. Judah b. Beteira – a rabbi in the diaspora! – the priests are incapable of protecting the sacred.[150]

Let us ignore the fictional and polemical nature of the story and put ourselves in the priests' position. According to the book of Acts Paul was accused of bringing a gentile into the temple; whether the accusation is true we do not know.[151] According to this rabbinic story a gentile was able to deceive the priests (and apparently all the Jews around him) and to partake of the Passover. The priests were the custodians of the temple, but they could hardly be expected to check all those who entered the sacred precincts, certainly not at the pilgrimage festivals when the crowds were immense. The Pauline episode apparently took place at or around the time of Pentecost (Acts 20:16). Passover in particular attracted large numbers of people. According to Josephus, Cestius Gallus once took a census and counted 255,600 Paschal sacrifices; according to the parallel rabbinic story, 600,000 Paschal sacrifices were counted. Both the rabbis and Josephus agree that on average each sacrifice was to serve a group (*havurah* in rabbinic parlance) of ten people. Thus, according to Josephus, there were at least 2,556,000 people in Jerusalem for the Passover, and according to the rabbis there were six million![152] These numbers do not include gentile visitors who came to watch the proceedings but could not participate.[153] So impressive were the proceedings that according to one rabbinic story Roman soldiers would convert on the 14th day of Nisan in order to be able to partake of the Paschal sacrifice in the evening.[154] Here, then, is a city teeming with native Judaeans, Jews from abroad, long-time converts and recent converts, gentile sightseers and gentile venerators of God – how were the priests to distinguish Jew from gentile, especially on the Passover when all the slaughtering and sacrificing had to be completed in the space of only several hours? Josephus even tells a story of one Passover when Samaritans took advantage of the confusion, slipped into the

---

[150]The deferential attitude of temple priests to rabbinic sages is a motif that appears elsewhere in rabbinic historiography, but neither the motif nor its historicity need to be investigated here.

[151]See appendix B.

[152]Josephus, *Jewish War* 6.423-425; Tosefta Pisha 4:15 p. 166 ed Lieberman; see Lieberman's commentary ad loc. Josephus and the rabbis agree that the Passover sacrifice was normally eaten by a group of ten or more; even R. Yosi, who permits Paschal sacrifices for individuals (M. Pesahim 8:7), would, I think, agree that individual sacrifices were not the norm.

[153]Josephus *Jewish War* 6.427; cf. John 12:20.

[154]Tosefta Pisha 7:14 p. 182 ed. Lieberman (and parallels; see Lieberman's commentary ad loc.).

temple, and scattered the dust of pulverized bones everywhere, seeking to render the temple impure.[155]

Gentiles were permitted to enter the temple mount, but were prohibited from entering the actual temple precincts (the *hieron*) which were marked off by a low balustrade (*soreg* in rabbinic parlance). A Greek inscription warned gentiles that they faced death if they violated the sacred precincts with their presence:[156]

> No gentile may enter within the screen and the enclosure around the temple. Whoever shall be caught (doing so), shall be responsible for his own death which follows.

The priests will have been entrusted with the duty of protecting the temple from foreign contagion, but in the final analysis, the priests did not keep gentiles out of the temple as much as well-intentioned and respectful gentiles kept themselves out of the temple. No doubt their good intentions and respectful attitude were strengthened by their fear – if caught they would die, as the inscription warned, whether by lynching or by judicial execution or by divine visitation.[157] No doubt gentiles who were determined to enter the temple could do so, just as Richard Francis Burton and other westerners have disguised themselves as Muslims and gone on pilgrimage to Mecca.[158] If a gentile knew how to pass as a Jew, and certainly if that gentile was in the company of a Jewish accomplice (like Paul), he (or she) would have had no difficulty in entering the temple precincts and/or joining a *havurah* to partake of the Paschal sacrifice.

The rabbinic story concludes that "They investigated him (literally: they investigated after him, *badqu batreh*) and they found that he was a gentile and they killed him." It is most unfortunate that the story does not explain how they investigated him or what exactly they investigated. Perhaps they checked to see whether or not he was circumcised – the gentile apparently was not circumcised, to judge from the glee with which he recited the prohibition *no uncircumcised person may eat of it* – but

---

[155]*Jewish Antiquities* 18.30; the text is corrupt and is variously construed.

[156]Schürer-Vermes 2:285 n. 57. D. R. Schwartz suggests that the inscription was meant to exclude converts as well as gentiles, and he may well be correct; see Schwartz, "On Two Aspects of a Priestly View of Descent at Qumran," *Archaeology and History in the Dead Sea Scrolls*, ed. Lawrence H. Schiffman (Sheffield: JSOT, 1990; JSEP Supp 8) 157-179 at 165-166.

[157]Peretz Segal, "The Penalty of the Warning Inscription from the Temple of Jerusalem," *Israel Exploration Journal* 39 (1989) 79-84. The story about Paul in Acts (see appendix B) suggests execution by lynching, whereas our rabbinic story suggests execution by judicial execution.

[158]Edward Rice, *Captain Sir Richard Francis Burton* (New York: Scribner's, 1990).

it is more likely that they investigated his pedigree.[159] As I discussed above there is no evidence that Jews checked circumcision as proof of Jewishness.[160]

Conclusions

"Thus are Israel: whithersoever one of them goes, he is unable to say that he is not a Jew. Why? because he is recognizable (or: because he is recognized, *shehu nikkar*)."[161] In the words of R. Abin, "A woman is able to hide herself (among gentiles) and say `I am a gentile,' but a man is unable to hide himself (among gentiles) and say `I am a gentile.'"[162] Unfortunately neither of these texts explains exactly what makes a Jew (at least a Jewish man) recognizable and unassimilable. In this paper I have argued that, rabbinic evidence to the contrary notwithstanding, the diaspora Jews of antiquity were not easily recognizable, if, indeed, they were recognizable at all. Jews looked like everyone else, dressed like everyone else, spoke like everyone else, had names and occupations like those of everyone else, and, in general, closely resembled their gentile neighbors. Even circumcision did not always make (male) Jews distinctive, and as long as they kept their pants on, it certainly did not make them recognizable. Like many other diaspora peoples ancient and modern, the Jews of antiquity maintained their identity without becoming conspicuous.

How, then, did you know a Jew in antiquity when you saw one? The answer is that you did not. But you could make reasonably plausible inferences from what you saw. First, if you saw someone associating with Jews, living in a (or the) Jewish part of town, and, in general, integrated socially with other Jews, you might reasonably conclude that that someone was a Jew. Second, if you saw someone performing Jewish rituals and practices, especially if the practice entailed an expenditure of

---

[159]Cf. M. Qiddushin 4:4-5. In its other occurrences on B. Pesahim 3b, the phrase *badqu batreh* clearly refers to genealogical investigation.

[160]Of course here there are two issues: "Jewishness" and circumcision. The two are not identical, because even an uncircumcised Jew who ate of the Paschal sacrifice would violate Exodus 12:48. See Mekilta Pisha 15 p. 57 ed. Horovitz-Rabin with the note ad loc.

[161]Song of Songs Rabbah on Song of Songs 6:11 (p. 35b ed. Vilna); cited by Salo Baron, "Problems of Jewish Identity," *Proceedings of the American Acadamey for Jewish Research* 46-47 (1979-1980) 33-67, at 52 n. 23.

[162]Y. Avodah Zarah 2:1 40c. The commentaries differ on the explanation for a man's inability to disguise himself; some say (see *Pilpula Harifta* on R. Asher, Avodah Zarah, chapter 2, paragraph 4) it is because of his circumcision, while others (see the *Pnei Moshe* in the Yerushalmi ad loc.) think it is because of his hair and beard.

money, you might reasonably conclude that that someone was a Jew. Each of these conclusions would have been reasonable, but neither would have been certain, because gentiles often mingled with Jews and some gentiles even observed Jewish rituals and practices. As a result, these reasonable conclusions would lead you to label some gentiles as Jews. Some ancient authors distinguish between "truly being a Jew" and "acting the part of a Jew," or between "truly being a Jew" and "being called a Jew." By observing Jewish practices and by associating with Jews, gentiles will have been called Jews and will have been mistaken as Jews.

Some gentiles will have been called Jews, others will have called themselves Jews. In situations where status as a Jew conferred privileges and/or esteem, that status will have been coveted by outsiders, and we may be sure that as a result some non-Jews converted to Judaism and others simply declared themselves to be Jews. The Jews of Rome and of the cities of Asia Minor and Syria enjoyed a wide range of legal privileges, and at times were socially and economically prominent; in the Roman legal system the Jews of Egypt occupied a place above that of Egyptians. In these environments gentiles would have had strong incentive to declare themselves to be Jews, and it would have been relatively easy for them to do so, especially in places where the Jewish community was large.

The Tosafot, medieval glossators on the Talmud, deduce from the Ben Beteira story cited above that if an unknown person comes before us and claims to be a Jew, he is to be believed.[163] This principle, still followed today in all but the most tightly knit Jewish communities, seems to have been the norm in antiquity not only in the land of Israel but also in the diaspora. In the book of Acts Paul travels throughout the eastern Mediterranean, preaching in synagogues and having discussions with local Jewish leaders, but not once is he asked to demonstrate his Jewishness or prove his Jewish identity.[164] Apparently he is accepted at his word immediately. Similarly, there are many stories about rabbis traveling throughout the ancient Mediterranean world, but, as far as I have been able to determine, they are never asked to identify themselves

---

[163]The Tosafot endorse this principle even if they conclude that our story does not provide conclusive support for it. See Pesahim 3b, Tosafot s.v. *va'ana* and the *Pisqe Tosafot*. With minor modifications the same argument appears also in the Tosafot of Sens, the Tosafot of R. Peretz, and the novellae of R. Yom-Tov ibn Ashvili (the Ritba) and R. Nissim of Gerona (the Ran); the texts are conveniently collected in *Gemara Shelemah*.

[164]Cf. Acts 28:21: the Jews of Rome know nothing of Paul or his message, but accept him immediately as a Jew. He is also immediately believed when he declares himself to be a Roman citizen; see above.

to their fellow Jews or to prove their Jewishness. In antiquity you did not know a Jew when you saw one, but if someone said he or she was a Jew, that statement alone apparently sufficed to establish the fact. A Jew is anyone who declares himself/herself to be one. In this respect as in so many others antiquity anticipates modernity.[165]

Appendix A: Two Epigrams of Martial

Martial has one explicit reference to Jewish circumcision and one implicit reference. The explicit reference is 7.30.5 = Stern #240, *nec recutitorum fugis inguina Iudaeorum;* the implicit reference is 11.94 = Stern #245, the four-fold repetition of *verpe poeta* in reference to someone born in Jerusalem. These passages are briefly discussed above. Stern sees two other references to circumcision in the epigrams of Martial, but in one case his interpretation is almost certainly wrong, and in the other the text is ambiguous.

In 7.35 = Stern #241, Martial contrasts the nominal modesty of Laecania, whose slave wears a thong while he attends upon her as she bathes, with his own nominal immodesty: *inguina succinctus nigra tibi servos aluta / stat, quotiens calidis tota foveris acquis. / sed meus, ut de me taceam, Laecania, servos / Iudaeum nulla* (or: *nuda*) *sub cute pondus habet.* "A slave, girt under his groin with a black leather strap, waits on you whenever you are heated all over with warm waters. But my slave, Laecania – to say nothing of myself – has a Jewish load under no skin (or: under bare skin)." The "black leather strap" is a thong that covers the penis.[166] "Jewish load" (or "Jewish weight") means that the slave has an unusually large penis. In 7.55 = Stern #242 Martial contrasts his own tiny organ (*pusilla est*) with the cock (*mentula*) of a man who has just come from Jerusalem. There Martial is following the topos that the "other" is characterized by large genitals and that a small penis is a sign of decent character.[167] Here, however, Martial is happy to speak of his own large organ ("to say nothing of myself"). The phrase *nulla sub cute* (the reading preferred by virtually all modern editors) or *nuda sub cute* (the reading preferred by Stern) is somewhat obscure. Reading *nulla sub cute,* A.E. Housman argues that *cutis* = foreskin, and that Martial means "my slave, who is Jewish, has a cock that is large and not even hidden by a

---

[165]Salo Baron, *History and Jewish Historians* (Philadelphia: Jewish Publication Society, 1964) 5-22 (an essay entitled "Who is a Jew?").

[166]Hall, "Epispasm," 73, erroneously thinks it a reference to infibulation.

[167]See Dover, *Greek Homosexuality* 127-129. That the Jews are particularly lusty see Tacitus cited below (*proiectissima ad libidinem gens ...inter se nihil illicitum*) and cf. Sullivan, *Martial* 189 n. 6.

foreskin."[168] Following Housman, Stern comments, "Martial alludes to his Jewish slave as being circumcised." *cutis* certainly can mean "foreskin" (see above), but Martial does not say that his slave was Jewish (it is not the *servos* but the *pondus* that is *Iudaeum*), and it is much simpler to take *cutis* as synonymous with *aluta*, meaning "leather." Laecania's slave wears a thong but my well-hung slave does not. Since Martial compares himself to his slave ("to say nothing of me"), it is most unlikely that he is describing his slave either as Jewish or as circumcised. My slave – to say nothing of me – has a large penis and does not hide it under a thong. This epigram has nothing to do with circumcision.

(If we adopt the reading *nuda*, *cutis* must mean foreskin and the epigram gains in ironic force: Laecania's slave wears a thong, but my slave – to say nothing of me! – has a large load, worthy of a Jew, under his bare foreskin. Whether *pondus* refers to the penis or the testicles, is not entirely clear. The irony is the juxtaposition of *Iudaeum* with *cutis*: Jews do not, or are not supposed to, have foreskins, but this slave combines a foreskin with a Jewish-sized *pondus*).

The interpretation of the second text turns on the ambiguous word *verpus*. Martial 7.82 = Stern #243 describes a comic actor or singer, one Menophilus, who wore a fibula, ostensibly to protect his voice. While he was exercising in public, however, his fibula fell off, revealing to everyone that he was *verpus*. A fibula is a pin or a ring worn through the foreskin and designed to make erection either painful or impossible. The infibulated man would thus abstain from sex and thereby (it was believed) improve his voice and/or his strength.[169] The epigram can be construed in two ways. "I had thought that Menophilus wore a fibula in order to spare his voice, but now that his fibula fell out in public I realize that he wore it to hide his circumcision." This is how the epigram has usually been understood.[170] However, there is an alternative. "I had thought that Menophilus wore a fibula in order to spare his voice, but now that his fibula fell out in public I realize that he wore it to restrain his agressive and unseemly homosexual lust" (that is, his fibula fell out when he had an enormous erection). *verpa* means erection in Martial 11.46. Perhaps both meanings are intended here as in 11.94 (*verpe poeta*). If Menophilus was circumcised and had no foreskin, how did he affix a fibula? If Menophilus was circumcised and still managed to affix a

---

[168]Housman, "Praefanda," *Hermes* 66 (1931) 402-412, at 409-410. Housman is followed by Adams 73.

[169]Kay, *Martial Book XI*, 229-231 (commentary on 11.75).

[170]See for example Stern, commentary ad loc.; Smallwood, *Jews* 377; Kay 229; Hall, "Epispasm," 73; Williams, "Domitian," 203.

fibula, it is easy to see how it might have fallen off! It is not clear if this epigram has anything to do with circumcision.

Sullivan, *Martial* 189, writes "There are a number of sneers (for example 7.82) at those *verpi* ('skin-backs') who have been circumcised by their masters in order to gratify their perverse sexual tastes." I have been unable to verify this statement. Neither 7.82 nor 11.94, the only two passages in Martial to use the word *verpus*, refers to slaves who were circumcised in order to gratify their masters' perverse sexual tastes. I know of no references to circumcision in Martial aside from those discussed here and in the text above.[171]

Appendix B: Paul and Trophimus in the Temple:

Acts 21:27-29 reports the following:

> When the seven days [of the purification of the Nazirites] were almost completed, the Jews from Asia, who had seen him [Paul] in the temple, stirred up all the crowd, and laid hands on him, crying out, "Men of Israel, help! This is the man who is teaching men everywhere against the people and the law and this place; moreover, he also brought Greeks into the temple, and he has defiled this holy place." For they had previously seen Trophimus the Ephesian with him in the city, and they supposed that Paul had brought him into the temple. Then all the city was aroused, and the people ran together; they seized Paul and dragged him out of the temple, and at once the gates were shut.

Paul is almost beaten to death by the crowd, but is arrested (and thus rescued) by Roman troops, and after a long series of interviews and hearings is sent off to Rome for trial before the emperor.

Paul is the target of two separate accusations: first, of teaching against the people (that is, against the Jews), against the law (that is, against the laws of the Torah), and against the place (that is, against the temple); second, of bringing Greeks, that is, gentiles, into the temple, thereby defiling it. Acts, of course, implies that both accusations are false, but anyone who has read the Pauline epistles, especially Galatians, will have to concede that the first accusation, at least, has merit. Against this accusation the Paul of Acts speaks eloquently of his Jewish upbringing, his loyalty to Jews and and Judaism, and his "conversion." But it is the second accusation that concerns us here. Acts explains that the accusation arose because Paul had been seen in the city with Trophimus of Ephesus, a man thought to be a gentile, and the Jews of Asia Minor, themselves, like Paul, pilgrims to the holy city, were

---

[171]Prof. Sullivan, in response to my query about the meaning of his statement, was kind enough to send me a detailed explanation which I do not find persuasive. I hope to return to this point elsewhere.

convinced that Paul had brought Trophimus into the temple. Trophimus and any other alleged gentiles allegedly introduced into the temple by Paul were certainly liable to be killed if apprehended (see above). Presumably they were nowhere to be found; the mob turned its anger instead against Paul.

How does Paul respond to this accusation? He ignores it. In the subsequent narrative the accusation is mentioned again in 24:6 by one of Paul's prosecutors, but Paul does not deign to reply. "Let my accusers (the Jews of Asia) confront me directly," he says (24:19). The accusation that Paul introduced gentiles into the temple is probably pre-Lucan tradition (that is, Luke, the author of Acts, did not invent it but learned of it from one of his sources[172]), and it is striking, then, that Luke (or his source) did not see fit to record Paul's response, especially if Paul's response would have been "I did not bring Trophimus or any other gentile into the temple." Perhaps Acts suppresses Paul's defense because the defense would not have accorded well with Act's picture of a Jewishly-pious and non-antinomian Paul. Perhaps Paul would have said "I brought Trophimus, a gentile, into the temple, but the distinction between Jew and gentile no longer exists in God's eyes, and gentiles may worship freely in the house of God just as Jews do." If this was Paul's defense one can understand why Luke would have supppresed it, because it would have run counter to his image of a Paul who never speaks the sort of theology that is central to Galatians.[173]

There is yet a third way in which Paul might have responded to the accusation. He might have said, "Yes, I brought Trophimus into the temple, but Trophimus is really a Jew, not a gentile." This response is full of uncertainties, for how would the Jews of Asia Minor have attempted to prove Trophimus to be a gentile, and how would Paul have attempted to prove him to be a Jew? Presumably everyone would have checked Trophimus' genealogy, or would have asked him to verify that he was a convert. Perhaps they would have checked his circumcision (or perhaps not; see above). If this was Paul's defense, we may imagine that it was suppressed by Luke because Luke had no doubt that Trophimus was indeed a gentile. In any case, this story, like the Ben Beteira story cited above, shows that even in connection with the one Jewish institution that required clear distinction between Jews and gentiles,

---

[172]This seems to be the general consensus; see Gerd Lüdemann, *Das frühe Christentum nach den Traditionen der Apostelgeschichte* (Göttingen: Vandenhoeck & Ruprecht, 1987) 243-244.

[173]Morton Smith, "The Reason for the Persecution of Paul and the Obscurity of Acts," *Studies in Mysticism and Religion presented to Gershom Scholem* (Jerusalem: Magnes, 1967) 261-268.

Jewish identity was not always easy to determine and separation between Jews and gentiles was not always easy to enforce.

2

The Unromanized in Rome

Ramsay MacMullen

One day in Caracalla's reign in Rome, a sort of shouting match broke out in the Circus Maximus between the spectators who were of senatorial or equestrian rank, and all the rest of the people. It was conducted in Greek, as Dio specifies (79.20.2). He may have been present. At the same period, as earlier, the Christian community in the city conducted its business in Greek, not Latin. The same can be said of the city's several Jewish communities as well as the worshippers of Sarapis centered in the great temple on the Campus Martius or the lesser one on the Quirinal; likewise, congregations around several other gods, Kore, Asclepius, Dionysus, and others. The imperial medical college used Greek as the most natural language for an inscription, not surprisingly, given the origins of their art; but it is less expected that public honor in the city should be paid to patrons and patronesses in Greek, by their grateful dependents. It was in Greek, too, that urban precinct chiefs, *magistri*, proclaimed their loyalty to the emperor Septimius Severus. They would be freedmen, explaining the choice. Finally, to secure their burial plots in perpetuity, many deceased asserted their claims to the world at large in Greek, confident that officialdom as well as the passer-by would take due notice; and notice of similar legal claims was posted up in Greek on the walls of one of the great public warehouses by a renter asserting his rights. The people commissioning these statements, or their ancestors, had originated in the Hellenized provinces, mostly from Asia Minor and Syria; but despite their years in the city, they had not been fully absorbed into, nor did they themselves absorb, the strange ways around them.

47

What is evident, further, is the degree to which they assumed that the city round them shared their culture.[1]

For the foreign-ness of Rome, language is not the only proof or index; but it is a particularly informative one, allowing us as it does to include in our assessment the masses who are so seldom heard from in our literary sources. Some very significant minority of the capital, even after many generations, had not become thoroughly Romanized – among them, in illustration, one who commissioned a plaque to be set up in Greek "to Aglibol and Malachbel, ancestral deities, with a fully ornamented silver statuette." The dedicant added his name in Palmyrene: he was Iarhai son of Haliphi, son of Iarhai, son of Lisams, son of Soadu.[2]

Of such alien figures as Iarhai, explanation must be sought first in the broad social context of their life experience. We have, let us suppose, some three quarters of a million resident in Rome at the point in time when our examination begins, in the reign of Augustus, increasing to a round million over the next century and a half.[3] The terminology of

---

[1]For sources, see W.H.C. Frend, *The Rise of Christianity* (1984) 338, the church Greek speaking till ca. 240; R. MacMullen, *Changes in the Roman Empire* (1990) 345; and L. Moretti, *Inscriptiones Graecae Urbis Romae* (*IGUR*) (1968-1990). M. Dubuisson, "Le Grec à Rome à l'époque de Cicéron," *Annales E.S.C.* 47 (1992) 187-206, reports on an earlier period than concerns me and, besides (191ff.), concerns himself explicitly with the elite classes only. For the association of physicians in the imperial *familia*, see *IGUR* 30, of the AD 180s; for Serapis-cult colleges, see *IGUR* 25 (Caracalla's reign), 77 (AD 146) and 35 (with W. Williams, "Epigraphic texts of imperial subscripts," *ZPE* 66 [1986] 190f.), and *IGUR* 190 (dedication to Caracalla by a priest); add Kore-cult members (86), Asclepius worshippers on the Esquiline (104), Dionysus worshippers often, including the well-known association under Agrippinilla (160, plus 157f.); and below, on Trastevere cult groups, nn. 34f. For patron(ess)-dedications, see *IGUR* 1045 and others listed in the volumes' Index s.vv.; the *magistri* in 1659, cf. L. Moretti, "Vicus Canarius," *Rend. Pont. Accad. di Archeologia* 61 (1988-89) 355f., of Severan times, the provenience being in a district specially Christian, later; and public notices in *IGUR* 333, 432, 841, 1664, and 1692 (burial plots) and 413 from the *horrea Petroniana* on the Via Marmorata. Some sense of who the Greek inscribers were can be gained best from cognomina like "Antiochus;" but typical also are the indications of origin from Aphrodisias (*IGUR* 1368, 1598, 1627), Nicomedia (1429, 1430, 1475, 1766), Laodiceia (1569, 2047, 2148), Smyrna (1601, 2003), Stratoniceia (1484), Limyra (Lycia: 2068), Side (1702), Pontus (1374, 1787), and Syrians like the dedicants of 1661 and 1728 (with some of the Laodiceans). One Syrian specifies his trade as *marmorarios* (1443); another Greek dedicant is a *vestiarios* (1686).
[2]*IGUR* 119 of AD 236.
[3]P.A. Brunt, *Italian Manpower* (1971) 383, for the period of Augustus; G. Alföldy, *Römische Sozialgeschichte*³ (1984) 88, a million in the Principate; or F. Vittinghoff in the *Handbuch der Europäischen Wirtschafts – und Sozialgeschichte* I (1990) 21, "eine

housing invites us to imagine a population made up of a tiny elite atop the masses, as if there were no middle class at all.[4] There existed in both common and official use the two terms *domus,* meaning mansions, and *insulae,* meaning apartment buildings. Granted, within the two types of housing there was no absolute uniformity; but both are distinguishable on Rome's ancient municipal map, the so-called Marble Plan of around AD 200, as they were distinguishable also to the compilers of the early fourth century urban architectural inventories called Regionaries. They may, then, fairly serve to organize what evidence survives about the indigestible masses.

The Regionaries list 1,797 *domus* and 46,602 *insulae;* but the latter total has been challenged head-on, and is likely to have been much smaller.[5] Across the ancient city as a whole, the houses of the rich and poor were jumbled together in considerable confusion. There were of course the more and the less desirable regions to live in, correspondingly sought out: in particular, the Palatine hilltop, preserve of the very rich at an early date, and later, of the imperial palaces. But *domus* and *insulae* nevertheless should be seen as expressions in brick of broad social distinctions, representing an inner and an outer urban ring not so much in physical position as in their residents' closeness to the centers of power, wealth, and prestige.

In addition, *domus* serve to introduce another distinction, that of civic status within the masses: great numbers of the whole population were slaves, of whom in turn perhaps a half served the aristocracy in its grand residences, living packed in to basement rooms and odd crannies.[6] In

---

communis opinio auf etwa 600 000 bis ein Million" for the same period. I would regard these estimates as maxima, but there is no reason here to discuss the point.

[4]"There is no evidence for a middle class in the city..., except for some rich freedmen," says Brunt l.c. – which is clearly wrong. Even if "class" is defined only in money terms, there is good evidence for people of intermediate wealth measured in terms of place of residence: Martial, for one (*Epigrams* 1.108.3), with more in B.W. Frier, *Landlords and Tenants in Imperial Rome* (1980) 39-47; nor can we believe that the more spacious second floor accommodations of *insulae,* contrasted with the upper floor cubicles, did not represent an economic stratum. See J. Packer, "La casa di via Giulio Romano," *Bull. Comm.* 81 (1968-69) 132ff. and passim. But I agree with Frier (p. 65) that "the lower classes obviously made up the huge majority of this tenantry."

[5]G. Lugli, *Studi minori di topografia antica* (1965) 79; idem, "Il valore topografico e giuridico dell' 'insula' in Roma antica," *Rend. Pont. Accad. Arch.*[3] 18 (1941-42) 202ff., defining the term insula and (208) reducing the totals to ca. 40,000; G. Hermansen, "The population of imperial Rome: the Regionaries," *Historia* 27 (1978) 167, reducing the likely number to 25,000.

[6]I sketched what I thought were likely proportions for Augustus' reign in *Changes in the Roman Empire* (1990) 327 – no more than a guess, yet given boundaries by a great deal of anecdotal information, e.g. Val. Max 4.3.12 (a retinue of only a dozen

absolute figures (if we accept the total of *domus* in the written sources), slaves owned by senators and by those rich equestrians who chose to reside in the capital may have numbered some 100,000. To these should be added several thousands more in the grandest *domus* of all, those built by and for the emperors. It is on this population of domestic slaves and their manner of life that we should concentrate first.

From time to time they might be released into the city's streets, shops, and apartments, or into its cemeteries, through manumission or death, those lost being replaced by an equal number through birth within the home or importation from beyond Italy. Among the latter we have our first glimpse of Greek speaking immigrants. Roman masters and mistresses preferred people who, in civilization and appearance, fitted in to the household. So much we may imagine, in order to explain known facts. For Celts and Copts and their like were not much wanted for domestic service, in contrast to persons from the relatively urbanized, Hellenized areas of what had been the Seleucid empire: Syria or Asia or Lycia and Pamphylia.[7] An illustration of the preferences at work may be found in a dedication set up by a freedman (so it is safe to say), C. Granius Hilarus, to Jupiter, to the Dea Syria, and to the guardian angel of the slave trade.[8] The family of the Granii is well known, from which he was freed, "Joyful," as his name tells us, because he had so successfully introduced so many of the children of Atargatis to the Romans' great god, in chains.

The servant population of *domus* would constitute tiny societies of their own, confirmed at the end by the burial of many of them in each

---

slaves is exaggeratedly modest in Caesar's day), the term *nationes* chosen by Tacitus (*Ann.* 3.53) to describe the totals of senators' household staffs, or other reff. in F.G. Maier, "Römische Bevölkerungsgeschichte und Inschriftenstatistik," *Historia* 2 (1953-54) 337; totals of slaves, ibid., with Lugli, cit. (above, n. 1) 80. G. Calza, "La statistica delle abitazioni e il calcolo della popolazione in Roma imperiale," *Rend. Accad. naz. dei Lincei*[5] 26 (1917) 75, posits an average of 100 persons per *domus*, representing 4-5,000 families, which is not incompatible with my assumptions though arrived at from entirely different directions. The possible bibliography on the demography of Rome is huge.

[7]On the ethnic mix of the Roman servile population there has been much debate; but see a recent statement as typical, in W.V. Harris, "Towards a study of the Roman slave trade," *Roman Seaborne Commerce (Memoirs of the Am. Acad. in Rome XXXVI, 1980)* 122, pointing to Asia Minor as "the great source." Syria and Palestine were not far behind. For the origins specifically of domestic servants, see W. Boese, "A Study of the Slave Trade and the Sources of Slaves in the Roman Republic and the Early Roman Empire," Diss. University of Washington 1973, 123.

[8]*CIL* 6.399, where "I.O.M." is likely to be Haddad to match Atargatis, the Syrian goddess, here joined to the *genius venalicii*. The inscription's findspot in the city is uncertain.

family's particular vault. During the term of their service, it is safe to imagine them speaking their native language "below-stairs." The major-domo in charge of recruiting new members under him would not wish to introduce new nationalities, and his employers would of course know Greek, themselves; so a life of service in such a household need do little to inculcate Latin or Roman ways. From whom must they be learned? This is not to say that Greek speaking slaves for convenience' or ambition's sake did not often acquire the master tongue. It is less likely that they adopted the religious beliefs, child-rearing customs, manners, or core values of their master's or mistress' class.

For the imported or immigrant population, *domus* constituted so many little islands of security, compared at least with a more chancy life among the next ring of population to be considered: namely, persons engaged in trade and manufacture and lodged in *insulae*. They, too, and to a very large degree, perhaps over ninety per cent, were slaves or former slaves.[9] Rates of manumission from domestic service were such that the men and women bought for it and surviving into their later twenties or thirties could expect to gain their freedom at some point during those years, or soon after – could expect it, though as a favor not granted automatically, or to all.[10] Thereafter they were on their own, to the degree that they were not, as a condition of freedom, still obliged to contribute some portion of their work or profits to their former owners. Just what percentage may have gained their freedom is not an essential matter, here. What is needed is some sense of where all the city's small shopkeepers and artisans came from. It is not easy to imagine them as Italians originating in a rural environment, where they could hardly

---

[9]As to the lodging of slaves and freed, note *CIL* 6.1248 and 10239, in Lugli, "Valore topografico" (cit., n.5) 202f., both inscriptions showing an *insula* bequeathed to a man's freedmen. As to artisans, S.M. Treggiari, "Urban labour in Rome: *mercennarii* and *tabernarii*," *Non-Slave Labour in the Greco-Roman World* (1980) 55, finds half of the epigraphically attested *opifices* to be freed, some smaller number still in servitude; 52ff., texts on *tabernae* given in charge of slaves by their masters; and some further illustrative texts along with general remarks on manumission probabilities in P. Veyne, *La société romaine* (1990) 24. *Dig.* 30.1.36, 32.61, 35.1.17.1, and 36.1.80(78) all indicate the ownership of *textores* or *sutores,* who might be passed on by will.

[10]The rate of manumission is much controverted, but, between concentrating on the likelihood from out of *domus* employment, and heeding the arguments of L.R. Taylor, "Freedmen and freeborn in the epitaphs of imperial Rome," *AJP* 82 (1961) 116ff., the high-end estimates seem to me the preferable. G. Alföldy argued for a high rate in a striking study, "Die Freilassung von Sklaven und die Struktur der Sklaverei in der römischen Kaiserzeit" (1972), conveniently reprinted but with changes of 1981 in his *Die römische Gesellschaft* (1986) 286ff., including the *Nachträge* of 1980 and 1985, pp. 319-31, esp. 327-29.

acquire the skills in trade, in manufacture, and in general survival that the metropolis required. Juvenal in one of his *Satires* supplies a good illustration of the difficulties his rustic or small-town countrymen encountered in Rome.[11] It was not a friendly city.

People making or selling various articles declared themselves on inscriptions, providing us with most of our information about ordinary forms of livelihood. Adding mentions in literary sources, we can determine some of the commercial character of the Vicus Tuscus,[12] the Velabrum,[13] the Meat Market (*Forum Boarium*),[14] the Sacra Via,[15] and the Subura.[16] These are given as their home address by sellers of various foods, fabrics, and so forth. The Marble Plan confirms the literary picture of these districts as congested and commercial, with a high ratio of apartments to mansions. In both, especially in apartments, the ground floor along the streetside would be rented out for shops, just as one can see them today. At the rear lived the lessee and his or her family. The space was often maximized by creating a loft for sleeping – without light or air, barely habitable quarters. Slaves, however, and former slaves and their children familiar with the dark dormitories and makeshift crannies assigned them while in their masters' grand houses, may not have seen their life on their own as much worse.

Besides the districts just named, the Esquiline likewise had a great deal of poor housing.[17] The rich didn't want to live there because it was at so unfashionable a distance from the Forum; and besides, much of it

---

[11]Juv. 3.21ff; cf. Hor., *Sat.* 2.6.23-31.

[12]Hor., *Sat.* 2.3.228f., the *impia turba Tusci vici,* "godless" implying Jews? Also, *CIL* 6.33923, a freedman *vestiarius tenuiarius de vico Tusco.*

[13]In general, see G. Lugli, *Roma antica. Il centro munumentale* (1946) 591, citing *CIL* 6.467, an association of the Velabrenses; 9184, an *argentarius;* 9993, a freedman *vinarius;* 33933, a free or freed *turarius;* 9256, a slave *clavarius;* and a *negotiator penoris et vinorum de Velabro,* in R.E.A. Palmer, "The *Vici Luccei* in the Forum Boarium," *Bull. Comm.* 85 (1976-77) 158. He goes on to quote Horace and Martial on the character of the district as "nothing but a food market."

[14]*CIL* 6.33936, an *olivarius.*

[15]*CIL* 6.33872, a freedman *margaritarius;* cf. further S. Panciera, "Tra epigrafia e topografia," *Archeologia classica* 22 (1970) 133, 135ff.

[16]*CIL* 6.33862, a freedman *inpilarius,* felt-worker (cf. *DE* s.v.), his name (Antiochus) suggesting his Syrian origin. This was, with Trastevere, "the most congested quarter" of Rome, cf. G. Calza (cit. above, n. 6) 67; Lugli (cit., n. 5) 79; G. LaPiana, "Foreign groups in Rome during the first centuries of the empire," *HThR* 20 (1927) 210 n. 41; S. Collon, "Remarques sur les quartiers juifs de la Rome antique," *MEFR* 57 (1940) 87; or H.J. Leon, *The Jews of Ancient Rome* (1960) 152.

[17]On the unique degree of Esquiline crowding, see G. Calza (cit. above, n. 6) 67, and G. Pisani Sartorio, "L'Esquilino nell'antichità," *L'archeologia in Roma capitale tra sterro e scavo* (1983) 105.

lying beyond the city's primitive boundaries had been taken over for
pauper burials and for the housing of such outcasts as gravediggers. The
authorities had established a place for the execution of the indigent on
the edge of the Esquiline, the so-called Sessorium,[18] and had dug huge
pits just outside the pomerium a little to the north, to serve as mass
graves. *Puticuli*, these were called. Back in the 1870s, excavation
uncovered scores of them and their still stinking contents.[19] Still further
north along the curve of the old "Servian" Wall, the great ditch had been
used for paupers' graves over generations, probably centuries, until
reclaimed for his pleasure gardens by Maecenas. On the Esquiline Field
nearby, the disposing of corpses had been forbidden by a senatorial
decree.[20] Horace writes (*Sat.* 1.8.8f.), "Here once a fellow slave
contracted to transport the castaway corpses to narrow rooms on a cheap
chest; here lay the common grave of the wretched masses."

Because of religious taboos and the disgusting nature of the job, the
disposing of the bodies of slaves and the indigent fell to people utterly
rejected by the world.[21] That appears in regulations at Puteoli forbidding
them so much as to wash themselves when other folk were doing so, and
never to enter the city except when identified by a colored hat and the
sound of a bell they were to carry. The men most easily recruited into
such exiled status were the very young (mere boys), the very old, those
with open sores, half-blind, maimed, lame, branded – all specified as
categories that a contractor was most likely, but was forbidden, to use for

---

[18]On the Sessorium, see Plut., *Galba* 28, and Tac., *Ann.* 15.60.

[19]R. Lanciani, *Ancient and Modern Rome* (n.d.) 19, having excavated about 75 of the
pits, averaging 12 feet square, 30 deep; J. LeGall, "La sépulture des pauvres à
Rome," *BSNAF* 1980-81, 148f.; M. Albertoni, "La necropoli Esquilina arcaica e
repubblicana," *L'archeologia in Roma capitale tra sterro e scavo* (1983) 140; Pisani
Sartorio (cit., n.17) 102.; and N. Purcell, "Tomb and suburb," *Römische
Gräberstrassen*, eds. H. von Hesberg and P. Zanker (1987) 36, gathering reff. to the
physical appearance of city-edge slums, and rightly terming the graves
"notorious."

[20]Lanciani, *Ancient and Modern Rome*, cit., 20, and *Ancient Rome in the Light of
Recent Discoveries* (1888) 65, on excavation of a section of the *agger* 160 feet long,
100 wide, 30 deep, with room for perhaps 24,000 bodies; ref. also to the *cippi* of ca.
80 BC and AD 69 posted nearby, to ban cremations, burials, and refuse disposal;
the relevant texts in *FIRA*[2] 1.273 and 306f., with further discussion by LeGall l. c.;
and the indication in Varro, *L. l.* 5.25.3-4, that similar *puticuli* lay outside other
Italian cities.

[21]L. Bove, "Due nuovi iscrizioni di Pozzuoli e Cuma," *Rend. Accad. di Arch. e
Lettere e Belle Arti*[2] (1966) 215, from which I quote the provisions applying to
gravediggers in Puteoli. See also *FIRA*[2] 1.148, forbidding *quei libitinam faciet* to
run for municipal office, and Juv. 3.32, listing among the most wretched and
abandoned people the gatherers of corpses.

the job; and the same may be imagined as making up a part of the population, barely alive, that lodged in shacks and tombs around the edges of the city. Theirs was the outermost ring of the urban population, beyond the central city apartments.

It was on this undesirable periphery of Rome that certain synagogues developed (Fig. 1: Collon). In the city as a whole, the Jewish population has been estimated at 40,000-50,000. They were generally poor. Some concentrations of them are attested in the Subura, already encountered in its squalor; others, along the *agger* of the "Servian" Wall and elsewhere near it, the most unpleasant of places to live: for example, in the neighborhood of the Porta Esquilina and Porta Capena.[22] The latter community is described by Juvenal (3.13f.) as made up of the wretchedly poverty-stricken, people possessed of only a bag of straw for a bed and a basket to hold all they owned. It is not surprising that an ethnic group well known for their poverty should seek out a life among their socioeconomic kind. It would bring them to the city's third ring, where the homeless settled, where the dead were disposed of, and where noxious industries were relegated. Among these on the Esquiline were, for example, lime-burners (*calcarienses*).[23]

On the other side of the city, it was not the Wall but the Tiber that marked the boundary between the better part of the citizenry, and the worse. It was known as the home of "the vagabond Trastevere man who trades pale sulphur-dipped kindling for broken glass," "the Jew taught by his mother to beg, and the half-blind seller of sulphur-dipped

---

[22]S. Collon, "Remarques sur les quartiers juifs de la Rome antique," *MEFR* 57 (1940) 78, 86, on numbers; for the Esquiline and Porta Capena and Porta Collina synagogues, ibid. 89f.; H.J. Leon, *The Jews of Ancient Rome* (1960) 45, the Jews "a large element in the population of the city," estimated at 20-60,000 (p. 135 n. 1), with ref. to the residents "of the *agger*," p. 139; further, E. Schürer, *The History of the Jewish People*, rev. ed. (1986) 3, 1, pp.96f., and E.M. Smallwood, *The Jews under Roman Rule* (1976) 521.

[23]*DE* s.v. Calcarienses, some organized in a *collegium*; J.P. Waltzing, *Étude historique sur les corporations professionnelles* 2 (1896) 116. Cf. *FIRA*[2] 1.184 (§76 of the *Lex Iulia municipalis*) forbidding large pottery works too near residential districts.

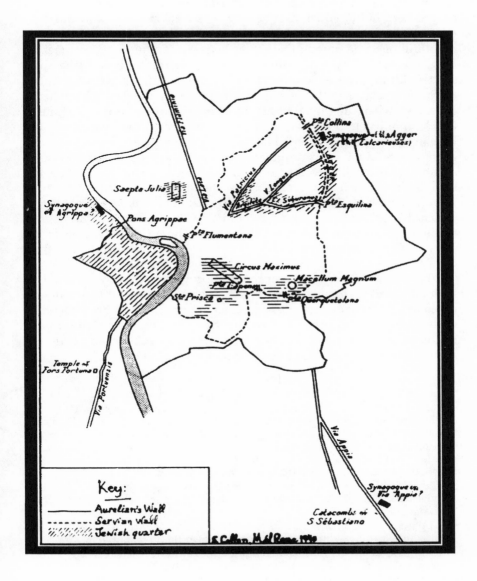

Figure 1

wares."[24] Martial whose verses are quoted had observed the beggar population of the city with a keen eye, and only wishes upon his worst enemy such a lot as theirs: "Let him wander an exile from the town's bridges and hills," which drew beggars because the foot- and carriage-traffic slowed down just there; "let him at the end beseech a dog's mouthful of bread among the hoarse beggars. To him let December be long and winter wet and the closing off of the archway [that had sheltered him] prolong a bitter chill. Let him call after the bodies, borne to paupers' graves on Hells' Barrow, that they are the blessed, the lucky ones. But when the thread of his final hours is spun, his day is come at last, let him listen to the dogs quarreling over which shall have him, and let him by flapping his ragged clothing drive off the evil birds." To this grim picture of the city's desperate, a single painting provides a striking addition (Fig. 2: Jahn).[25] It shows a man clothed in rags, half-naked, led by a dog on a leash. He reaches out his hand to a woman attended by a servant, while she offers him a little gift. Authors of the first century, to which this belongs, remark on the indigent in the streets of Rome as a familiar sight, even in the center, though their home lay in the outer ring. They would commute from Trastevere across the city's bridges, to their days' work as panhandlers and prostitutes.

Trastevere, the west side of the third ring, provided the central city with far more essential services (Fig. 3). It was, to begin with, a home for necessary but noxious neighbors, meaning potteries and brick-factories with their smoking ovens and tanneries with their stinking vats.[26] Beyond that, it provided the hands required to put food and drink on Roman tables. Romans did their shopping on the left bank, at the general

---

[24]Mart. 1.41.4 and 12.57.13f.; and I go on to quote 10.5.3f., cf. 12.32.10 and Juv. 4.116ff. and 6.542. L. Friedlaender, *Darstellungen aus der Sittengeschichte Roms*[10] (1922) 1.160, adds a ref. to Sen., *De vita beata* 25.1, "Take me to the Pons Sublicius, throw me among the beggars, *egentes,* who stretch out their hands for some small offering." Juv. 3.65 adds prostitution as a resort of the Syrian immigrant, offered near the Circus Maximus, and Tac., *Ann.* 15.62 notices a freedwoman supporting herself by prostitution among the slaves and freedmen of the household.

[25]From Herculaneum, cf. O. Jahn, "Über Darstellungen des Handwerks und Handelsverkehrs auf antiken Wandgemälden," *Abh. Sächs. Gesellschafts* 5 (1870) 287f. and Taf.III, 6.

[26]F. Coarelli, *Guida archeologica di Roma* (1974) 308f. (notice the street Coraria Septimiana, leading west from the river between the Pons Sublicius and Pons Probi); idem, *Roma*[2] (Guida Archeologica Laterza, 1981) 356, seven big leather-tanning vats, a factory? On a production area at the Villa Sciarra for various ceramic and bronze articles, see C. Mocchegiani Carpano, "Interventi sulle relazioni," *L'Instrumentum domesticum di Ercolana e Pompeii* (1977) 173f., and idem, "Considerazione sul versante orientale del Gianicolo," *L'area del' 'santuario siriaco del Gianicolo'. Problemi archeologici* (1982) 25ff.

Figure 2

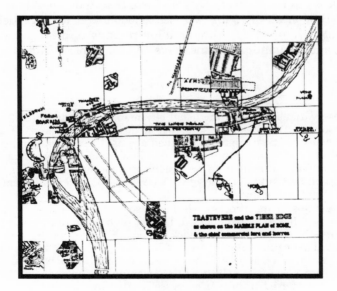

Figure 3

trade center (Emporium), the Meat Market, the Vegetable Market (Holitorium) just behind it, the Fish Market (Piscarium), and the Olive oil Market (Inter Olivarios) with its statue of Hercules the Olive Dealer, not to mention the Timber Market (Inter Lignarios) a little ways downstream, and the Masons' Market (Via Marmorata) still further along, next to the great public grain warehouses.[27] These essential, teeming, vital zones of commerce had no room to house their workers, who must all live in the cheap *insulae* across the river. There, there were some *domus* but not many, and mostly in the upper parts as semi-villas.

The gigantic mouth of Rome, as we may call the Tiber-side and its fora, needed the services of many hands indeed. We must first get the comestibles up-river from Ostia by hundreds of boats. They were moved partly by oar, by tugboats; mostly by haulers on the towpaths (Fig. 4: LeGall); and there was always some manufactured cargo by return trip to be loaded, too (Fig. 5: LeGall).[28] The varieties of labor can be seen in these two depictions, sketched to clarify the tiny, somewhat worn, reliefs on a statue of Father Tiber. The cargo depicted in reliefs and mosaics is generally in the form of sacks, chiefly of grain, and amphorae, chiefly of wine. Crews and haulers for such boats as were not based in Ostia numbered thousands; and there were boat builders and caulkers and marine divers in great numbers also, indicated by their organization into associations. Estimating a sack at 90 lbs and an amphora at around 100, some guess can be made at the work force required. To a daily need for some 150,000 *modii* of 15 lbs each, i.e. 25,000 loads, to be carried off the river boats, we must add three million pounds of meat per year, also attested, and a quantity of wine, olive oil, vegetables, fruits and spices

---

[27]For these various fora, see the usual city maps plus Palmer (cit., n. 13) 158. Notice (above, n. 1) a Greek speaking marble dealer, slave or freed, in one of the *horrea*. He and his type are to be weighed against the assumption by P. Brunt, which I do not disagree with, that the building trades in their great swings of employment drew far more from the free Italian poor than from slaves. See "Free labour and public works at Rome," *JRS* 70 (1980) 84, 87, and passim, emphasizing the great numbers employed.

[28]For depictions of the process, see L. Casson, "Harbour and river boats of ancient Rome," *JRS* 55 (1965) Plates II, 1, Tiber tugboat with rowers and hitch; II, 2, Ostian riverboat being loaded by sack bearers; II, 3, the same, but amphorae the cargo; III, 2, boat haulers at work in a Gallic river; V, 1, sack bearers unload boat, on a Campanian relief; and pp. 31 and passim, on numbers of boats, size of loads, etc.; R. Meiggs, *Roman Ostia* (1960) Pl.XXVIa, amphorae unloaded at Ostia; XXVa, amphorae transferred from marine vessel to riverine, on an Ostian mosaic; J. LeGall, "Les bas reliefs...," *RA* 21 (1944) Figs.2-3; idem, *Le Tibre* (1943) 230, misidentifying the process shown as off-loading into *horrea*.

Figure 4

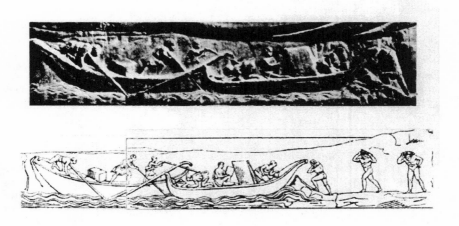

Figure 5

beyond estimating.[29]   An observer on the Mississippi in 1857 reported how "the steamboat arrives with, say, 10,000 bushels of grain. It comes in sacks – which have to be taken from the boat by a crowd of lazy laborers, who wearily carry it on their shoulders, sack by sack, and pile it on the levee.   [From] there...it has to be moved in drays...to a warehouse...where the same slow process has to be repeated....A hundred thousand bushels of grain in St. Louis involves the labor of probably two or three hundred Irishmen, negroes and mules for a couple of days."[30] Double the larger figure, that is, 600 men would be needed for Rome's food, just to get it off the boats.   They and their families account for some of the Trastevere population.

But it must next be stored – hence, some most typically Roman structures, absolutely gigantic and unashamedly useful: the Aemilian Portico backed by the Galbian Warehouse and behind that, the Lollian. They are easily reconstructed in the mind's eye thanks to the ground plan in Marble (Fig. 6: Gismondi).[31]   The larger was the Portico, of two

---

[29]Casson, l.c.; B. Sirks, *Food for Rome* (1991) 265, 269ff, 277, and 318 n. 52, assuming 250 mill owners in Rome milling 100 *modii* per day; 379, tonnage of meat; G. Rickman, *The Corn Supply of Ancient Rome* (1980) pp. xiii and 17-20., statistics of food supply reckoned in *modii* of ca. 9 liters = 1/4 bushel = 15 lbs, Rickman's estimates for the whole weight of grain, 40 million *modii* per year = 110,000 per day, being far lower than Sirks', and, I believe, closer to the truth, given usual estimates of required *modii* per year multiplied by the city's population. L. Casson, *Ships and Seamanship in the Ancient World* (1971) 172 nn. 23 and 25, reckons a grain *modius* at 13.6-13.75 lbs. For the weight of amphorae, see D. Manacorda, "Anfore spagnole a Pompei," *L'Instrumentum domesticum di Ercolano e Pompei nella prima età imperiale* (1977) 124f., from about 85 to 125 lbs when full.

[30]*Sixth Annual Rev. of the Commerce, Manufactures, and the Public and Private Improvements of Chicago* (Chicago 1858) 8. Ref. to a levee on the river edge is applicable to the Tiber, cf. Rickman 20 and LeGall, *Le Tibre* (cit., n.28) 118f. The grain volume mentioned in the St. Louis scene would make some 65,000 sacks, to be divided by 300 men X 2 days = 100 trips per man per day, five minutes per trip the day through.

[31]On the *horrea Galbana* or *Galbiana*, and *Lolliana*, see G. Gatti, "Frammento d'iscrizione contenente la *lex horreorum*," *Bull. Com.* 13 (1885) 112ff., concentrating on the epigraphy associated with the structures, including dedications set up by *horrearii* and esp. the rental regulations [now] *CIL* 6.33747 = *FIRA*[2] 3.455f., to which add *CIL* 14.20 on the *procurator ad oleum Galbae Ostiae Portus*, whose title indicates some of the contents of the building; *CIL* 6.33886, a freedman *marmorarius de Galbes*, 30983, a cult-*collegium* with a *vilicus praediorum Galbanorum*, and 30855 with various further texts there referred to, set up by *horrearii*, *saccarii*, and *operarii* of the three Galbian *cohortes*; Rickman 23, 45f., and 139f.; Sirks (cit., n. 29) 303; L. Crema, *L'architettura romana* (1959) 61 and 173, for bibliog.; G. Gatteschi, *Restauri della Roma imperiale* (1924) 19, showing an excellent reconstruction of the interior of the Horrea Agrippiana with workers in action.

Figure 6

Figure 7

stories, some 60 meters by nearly 500 (305 feet by 1,650) divided laterally into 50 bays on the ground floor. The bays themselves were divided into separate storage areas for rent. The adjoining Galbian had three courtyards with 140 storage bays and 225,000 square feet on the ground floor; and so on, for the other *horrea*, as they were called – a number of them identifiable by name and sometimes by location, and with few exceptions located close to the various fora they fed.[32] Indeed an entire administrative district of the church, the first Regio, was called "Horrea" because of the great number of warehouses for grain and other foods concentrated behind the Galbiana, and its underground burials are those of warehouse workers and longshoremen, their labors shown on their memorial frescoes (Fig. 7: Wilpert).[33] They had not only to take in and store at least six million sacks of grain per year, and as much bulk again in wine, oil, and other comestibles, but to dispense it again to retailers from the bays, rented as shops. Therefore, many thousands of men and of women, too.

In life, after their work, they had once trooped home each day across the Tiber, many hundreds of them, where they lived. The fact can be known not only from probability but from inscriptions. One in particular: found in what is now the Villa Sciarra far up the slopes of the Janiculan hill, an altar dedicated "To the Most Holy Sun" by a freedman, wife, and son, styling themselves "of the Third Cohort of the Galbensians."[34] They were all workers in one or another courtyard of the warehouse. Where the altar was found, thirty-odd dedications define the place as a shrine to eastern worships, Syrian, Arabian, Lebanese. The texts are in Latin, Greek, and Palmyrene, the latter suiting the district's community of that language. The whole of this vast Regio of the city was

---

[32]Lugli, *Roma antica* (cit., n.13) 535; S. Panciera, "Nuovi documenti epigrafici," *Rend. Pont. Accad. Rom, di Archeologia* 43 (1970-71) 110, 116-18; M. Conticello de'Spagnolis, *Il Tempio dei Dioscuri nel Circo Flaminio* (1984) 30ff. and Fig.1, two warehouses owned by women near the Tiber edge; and Palmer, *"Vici Luccei"* cit. (n. 13) 158ff.

[33]For ancient pictures of warehouse activity, see J. Wilpert, "Coemeteriale Fresken," *Römische Quartalschrift* 1887, Taf.III, 6, and idem, *Roma sotterranea. Le pitture delle catacombe romane* (1903) 485f. with Tav. 194f.

[34]The connection between the *horrea* and Trastevere's residents is seen, e.g., by E. Equini Schneider, "Il santuario de Bel...a Roma," *Dial. di Archeologia* 5 (1987) 69. For the Galbensians, see *ILS* 4337, often studied, most fully in context by R.E.A. Palmer, "Topography and social history of Rome's Trastevere (southern sector)," *Proc. Am. Philos. Soc.* 125 (1981) 376f. The presence of a woman among the Galbensian workers should not surprise – see *CIL* 6.9801, a woman fish seller *de horreis Galbae,* and Gatti's data (above, n. 9).

largely from the eastern Mediterranean.[35] Egyptian and Anatolian deities had their shrines here, dedicants bear names derived from eastern deities, a woman of Cyprus sets up a dedication, the emperor himself, Elagabalus of Syrian stock, here builds a Sun-temple, the main avenue along the Tiber is named after the totem animal of eastern worship, "Long Street of the Eagle," and in the graveyards to the south along the road to Portus and Ostia, the buried include a warehouseman in the Horrea Lolliana, among a number of Asian and Syrian freedmen and freed women, or again, nearby, warehousemen who depicted the Tiber docks on the frescoes of their tombs. Their names tell of Syrian and other eastern origins.

A last ethnic group and their cemetery remains to be mentioned: the Jews. It was in Trastevere that they first clustered; it was there they remained the largest and most undigested concentration among all their Roman coreligionists;[36] and there they continued the most faithful to their heritage, in such matters as the naming of children. Their inscriptions are more than three quarters in Greek, some in Hebrew, only a few in Latin. Mention of their community returns the discussion of immigrant indigestibility to its starting point – to language especially. That index served best to show the close limits around naturalization characterizing the Roman experience for immigrants of the early empire.

Now at the end, after laying out what can be known of that experience, it should be possible to explain its tendencies. The attempt cannot rise much above guesswork; but something reasonable emerges from putting together the epigraphic evidence, with which we started, and other evidence now assembled. As a first conjecture: there is no cause to think an individual from the eastern provinces was immersed in a society of Italians, within the mansions of the rich – the reverse is clear – nor, next, that within those other rings of *insulae* and of urban periphery there existed a critical mass of Italian poor to absorb and

---

[35]On the Oriental character of Trastevere, "a gigantic quarter," see e.g. Coarelli, *Guida* (cit., n. 26) 308 and 316ff.; LaPiana (cit., n. 16) 218ff., Trastevere "a region inhabited almost entirely by foreigners;" U. Bianchi, "Per la storia dei culti nel sito del' santuario siriaco sul Gianicolo," *L'area del santuario* (cit., n. 26) 91ff.; N. Goodhue, *The Lucus Furrinae and the Syrian Sanctuary on the Janiculum* (1975) 50, 131, and passim; G.W. Houston, "The altar from Rome with inscriptions to Sol and Malakbel," *Syria* 67 (1990) 189ff., whose view, however, that the *horrea Galbae* were apartment houses is not supported by the evidence (for the correct interpretation of the term *cohortes* see, e.g., *CIL* 6.30901 and other texts, above, n. 31); and Equini Schneider (cit. above, n. 34) 73, 89, and passim; but most full and useful by far is Palmer's, "Topography" (cit., n. 34), e.g. on the Via-Portuensis cemeteries at Pietra Papa (pp.385ff.) and, with its frescoes, at 'Ursus Pileatus" (394ff.).

[36]Collon (cit., n. 16) 77, 80, 83, and 85; Leon (cit., n. 16) 75ff., 110, 153, and 157.

dissolve the culture of foreigners living in their midst. It is doubtful, further, if the physical circumstances of immigrants in either *domus* or *insulae*, in all their poverty, presented them with a civilization they could readily adopt. What was most desirable around them would never be theirs – the luxury of their masters. What was theirs without their desiring it were their various stations of labor, at the lime-kiln, tow-path, tanning vat, dockside, warehouse, kitchen, or cook-shop. Between the unattainable and the too familiar there was indeed the space required for hopes; but it was occupied by temples to ancestral deities, addressed in Greek, even in Palmyrene and Hebrew. These places and the congregations there at home provided a haven to alien ways.

3

How to be a Jew in Hellenistic Egypt?

Joseph Mélèze Modrzejewski

I. – Semantic ambiguities and historical contingencies

The notion of "diaspora" is not a simple one.[1] That most venerable of all French encyclopedic dictionaries, the Larousse, considers the term as proper to religious history, and as limited to the Jewish people. I quote: "the dispersal, throughout the ancient world, of the Jews, driven from their country by the vicissitudes of history."[2] The more recent Hachette dictionary prolongs this dispersion in time: "throughout the centuries," and gives a second definition, by extension: "dispersal of some ethnic group," for example the Gypsy diaspora. This is, perhaps, not a happy choice. The French counterpart of the *Encyclopaedia Britannica*, the *Encyclopaedia Universalis*, correlates the rubric "Jews" with several others such as "ghetto," "Judaism," "Zionism;" it also offers us a

---

[1]This is an enlarged version of my paper presented to the Conference on "Diasporas in Antiquity" organized by Brown University, Providence, RI, on April 30, 1992, to celebrate the installation of Shaye J.D. Cohen as Samuel Ungerleider, Jr., Professor of Judaic Studies. I am thankful to Brown University for the invitation to take part in this Conference and for the hospitality I enjoyed in Providence. My best thanks are also due to my friends Robert Cornman, who prepared the English translation of my French original, and Nicholas de Lange, for valuable suggestions. To a large extent, this paper is based on material collected in my recent book *Les Juifs d'Égypte de Ramsès II à Hadrien*, Paris 1991 and 1992; on some points, it develops and specifies the views expressed there. Robert Cornman is now preparing an English version of this book to be published by the Jewish Publication Society, Philadelphia, in 1994.
[2]"Dispersion, à travers le monde antique, des juifs chassés de leur pays par les vicissitudes de leur histoire" (1948 edition).

more familiar definition: the Greek diaspora of modern times, a consequence of the Ottoman conquest of Greece, which touched off migrations to Western Europe, Asia, Africa and, later, America.[3] Other cases come to mind, and first of all that of the Armenians, who speak with pride and pain of their "Great Diaspora" of the nineteenth and twentieth centuries.[4] Nowadays the Palestinians have a tendency to promote theirs.

Thus it would seem that any people, deprived of the land it deems its own, a people strewn over the face of the earth, corresponds to the dictionary definition of a diaspora – with priority for the Jews. But this is a fragile conclusion. The homeland of the Gypsies has not been clearly determined. Before they were assigned an Indian origin (essentially for linguistic reasons), all sorts of hypotheses concerning them were bandied about. *Inter alia,* they were taken for a mixture of Jews and Moors, or for one of the lost Ten Tribes of Israel. Is this enough to qualify the Gypsies' wandering as a diaspora? On the other hand, no one has ever heard of a Polish diaspora, following the partitions of Poland among Russia, Prussia and Austria at the end of the eighteenth century. The Poles were not "dispersed," they "emigrated." The counterpart to the "Great Armenian Diaspora" is the "Great Polish Emigration" to France in the nineteenth century, followed by a new emigration to Great Britain and elsewhere after the Second World War. Is this rejection of the Jewish model to be interpreted as a manifestation of Polish anti-semitism, or should it simply lead to the conclusion that the word "diaspora" is not indefinitely extensible? The least one can say is that the notion is ambiguous.

Will etymology prove more useful to us than dictionaries or encyclopedias? *Diaspora* (διασπορά) stems from the Greek verb *diaspeirō* (διασπείρω), "to distribute," a compound of *speirō* (σπείρω), "to sow, to scatter like seed, to strew," and *dia-,* "from one end to the other." Curiously enough, for the ancient Greeks these Greek words did not apply to the migrations of the Greeks themselves. The various forms of the verb *diaspeirō* cut across two rather unrelated semantic fields: military operations and mental faculties. They can be used to describe the deployment of troops that are "spread about" or else ordered by ranks[5]; they also turn up in quite another context, as when Epicurus refers to "a dissipated soul"[6] or to a "widely held view" (a "current opinion" or a

---

[3]Vol. 18, 1974, p. 540-541.
[4]See e.g. G. Dedeyan, Ed., *Histoire des Arméniens,* Toulouse 1982, p. 377ff., 601ff.
[5]E.g. Thucydides, 1, 11; Xenophon, *Hellen.* 5, 3, 1
[6]Epicurus, *Epist.* 1, p. 21 U.

"consensus," in our modern jargon), τὸ διεσπαρμένον δόγμα.[7] In classical texts, the idea of the dispersal of a people does not come under this heading.

Nevertheless, the Greeks did not wait until the fall of Constantinople before launching out across the Mediterranean. During the early days of the city-state, between the eighth century BCE and the middle of the sixth, a great migratory movement carried them westwards, first to Sicily and southern Italy (Magna Graecia), then to the shores of the Black Sea and the coasts of Africa, Gaul and Spain. But neither in ancient days nor in ours has anyone ever referred to these peregrinations in terms of a diaspora, a "dispersion." To describe this phenomenon, today's practice is to speak of "colonization" – in truth, a rather inexact term, considering its modern connotations. In ancient times, terminology was centered around the notion of "emigration": *apoikein* (ἀποικεῖν), *apoikia* (ἀποικία) – literally: "to go away from home," "settlement far from home."[8] These are neutral expressions, indicating neither the cause of the displacement, nor its goal. Paradoxical neutrality: "cutting oneself off from home" is, *a priori*, a more dramatic act than "dispersing oneself."

Paradoxes of another kind appear in the vocabulary used by the Jews themselves. The word *diaspora*, now internationally consecrated, serves as an equivalent to the Hebrew notions of *galuth* (גָּלוּת) and *golah* (גּוֹלָה, גֹּלָה), derived from the verb *galah* (גָּלָה) expressing the ideas of deportation and exile. These two words originally meant, either exile in itself (*galuth*) or the collectivity of the exiled (*golah*), the nuance between them tending to disappear with time and custom. Here we are at the heart of those "vicissitudes of history" that swallowed up the ten tribes, led the Jewish people to captivity in Babylon and prolonged its dispersion throughout the world right up to our time. Thus *galuth* and *diaspora* co-existed and can still co-exist as synonyms.

This synonymy is not self-evident. In Biblical Hebrew, the word group closest to the Greek family *speirō* is not *golah* and its derivatives; it is made up of the verbal forms of the root *pe-vav-ṣade* (פוץ) which express the same idea of "dispersion." Modern Hebrew prefers this equivalence, which avoids the emotional overtones of *golah* and *galuth*. Although the feminine noun *tefuṣah*, the presumed equivalent of *diaspora*, is only attested once, in the plural, *tefuṣotēkhem* (תְּפוּצוֹתֵיכֶם), in a probably corrupt text of Jeremiah (Je 25, 34), its widespread use in Israel has consecrated

---

[7]Idem, *De rerum natura*, 14,7.
[8]See J. Seibert, *Metropolis und Apoikia. Historische Beiträge zur Geschichte ihrer gegenseitigen Beziehungen*, Würzburg 1963; A.J. Graham, *Colony and Mother City in Ancient Greece*, Manchester 1964.

the singular form *tefuṣah* (תְּפוּצָה), equivalent to "diaspora," as well as the plural *tefuṣot* (תְּפוּצוֹת), equivalent to "diasporas."

Still, in the Greek version of Jeremiah's text we just quoted, one could search in vain for the word *diaspora* (LXX Je 32, 34). For the Alexandrian translators the correspondence, *diaspora* = *tefuṣah* is not any more obvious than *diaspora* = *galuth*. Their terminology is governed by quite another logic.

When they deal with historical facts, they have recourse to the vocabulary of the Greek colonists. For them, exile is first and foremost an "emigration." They translate *golah* by *apoikia* (for example Je 29; LXX Je 36) or *apoikesia* (for example 2R 24, 15; LXX 4R 24, 15). In Ezra, the deportees, *bnē haggolah* (בְּנֵי־הַגּוֹלָה), are the "sons of the colony," *hoi hyioi tēs apoikesias* (οἱ υἱοὶ τῆς ἀποικεσίας: Ezr 6, 19; LXX 2 Ezr 6, 19). In the letter Jeremiah sent to "the elders of the golah," *ziqnē haggolah* (זִקְנֵי הַגּוֹלָה), these latter became "the elders of the colony," *presbyteroi tēs apoikias* (πρεσβύτεροι τῆς ἀποικίας: Je 29, 1; LXX Je 29, 1). The human collectivity that "the Lord caused to be deported (הִגְלֵיתִי) to Babylon" (Je 29, 4) becomes a colony (ἀποικία) which the Lord "made leave" Jerusalem (ἀπῴκισα: LXX Je 29, 4) in the fashion of a Greek *oikistes*, much as Battos, who led the colonists from Thera to the Libyan shores where they founded the city of Cyrene.[9] But Hecataeus of Abdera had already used the same term to present the conquest of the Promised Land as the establishment of a colony (ἀποικία) *à la grecque*. Hecataeus attributes this deed to Moses, whom he casts as the author of a *politeia* modeled partly on Platonic and partly on Spartan patterns, including the foundation of Jerusalem, its capital, and several other cities, the construction of the Temple, the grouping of the body of citizens into twelve tribes, the sharing of the land and the organization of an aristocratic government, in the hands of the priests.[10]

In the prophetic vision, other words come to the fore. The prophets abandon the vocabulary of colonization for the vocabulary of banishment. In Hebrew the key word is *nadah* (נָדַח) in its various forms: "scatter, chase apart, lead astray." Here the link between diaspora and exile is finally established. The translator of Deuteronomy breaks new ground for the meaning of the noun *diaspora*. In Dt 28, 25 he renders the Hebrew expression *le-za'awah* (לְזַעֲוָה) by *en diasporai* (ἐν διασπορᾷ): "thou

---

[9]Herodotus, 4, 145ff.; see M.B. Sakellariou, *Between Memory and Oblivion. The Transmission of Early Greek Historical Traditions*, Athens 1990, p. 38-65.

[10]Diod., *Bibl. hist.* 40, 3 *ap.* Photius, cod. 244: Th. Reinach, *Textes*, no. 9; M. Stern, *Authors*, no. 11. For a discussion of this passage, see Éd. Will, in Éd. Will & Cl. Orrieux, *Iudaïsmos – Hellènismos. Essai sur le judaïsme judéen à l'époque hellénistique*, Nancy 1986, p. 83ff.: "Les Juifs vus par Hécatée d'Abdère"; see also my article quoted below, note 74, p. 108ff. and 115ff. of the French version.

shalt be a horror" becomes "thou shalt be in the dispersion."[11] Further (Dt 30, 4), the same term *diaspora*, "dispersion," appears as the Greek equivalent to "banishment" (נִדַּחֲךָ). Isaiah's translator, in a text associating "banishment" and "dispersion" (Is 11, 12: LXX Is 11, 12), employs a participle of the verb *diaspeirō*: διεσπαρμένοι, for the "dispersed of Judea" (*nefuṣot Yehudah*, נְפֻצוֹת יְהוּדָה); for the "banished of Israel," *nidḥē Yisrael* (נִדְחֵי יִשְׂרָאֵל), he prefers a stronger verb, *apollymi* (ἀπόλλυμι), with the meaning of "snatched from one's homeland," *apolomenoi* (ἀπολόμενοι). But in Is 56, 8 *nidḥē Yisrael* becomes "dispersed," and in Psalm 146 (147), 2, "the diasporas of Israel."

It would be too easy to quibble with the Alexandrian Jews over their lexical choices. *Diaspora* and *diesparmenoi* are rather inadequate terms for "banishment" and "the banished." The Greeks were well acquainted with the notion of banishment as a penal sanction, for homicide, to begin with.[12] But here the verb *pheugein* (φεύγειν), "to flee," "to take the road to exile" was the common term, and not *diaspeirein*, "to disperse." The word that would apply to *nidhei Israel* is *phygades* (φυγάδες), "fugitives forced to flee," literally, "the banished." Ezekiel's translator seems to have understood this: in one manuscript of the Septuagint, explaining the allegory of the eagle and the vine (LXX Ez 17, 21, Rahlfs), he evokes the Babylonian captivity by the technical term for "banishment," *phygadeia* (φυγαδεία). This correct choice remains an isolated case. Other translators preferred "dispersion" to "flight."

Above and beyond this preference, the assimilation of the idea of captivity to that of colonization created a great gap between lexical data and the interpretation of historical reality. On this particular point, the Jewish experience appears indeed as the opposite of the Greek experience. The two peoples have in common the fact that a decisive period of their respective histories was placed under the sign of a great migratory movement. However, whereas Greek colonization at the dawn of the city-state took on the colors of a glorious adventure, the contemporary migrations of the Jews were the consequence of the multiple catastrophes which annihilated Israelite royalty, and culminated in the deportation of the entire people. Certainly, the Jews, too, had participated in voluntary migrations. This was the case in the fifth century BCE for the Judean colony of Elephantine in Egypt. Its origins go

---

[11]The same occurs later in Je 34, 17: LXX Je 41, 17. See the comments of R. Le Déaut, "La Septante, un Targum?", in R. Kuntzmann & J. Schlosser, Eds., *Études sur le judaïsme hellénistique*, Paris 1984, p. 147-195, esp. 174.

[12]M. Gagarin, *Drakon and Early Athenian Homicide Law*, New Haven & London 1981. Cf. G. Thür, Ztschr. Sav.-Stift., Rom. Abt. 102, 1985, p. 508-514, and my art. "La sanction de l'homicide en droit grec et hellénistique", in Symposion 1990, Cologne 1991, p. 3-16.

back to the 7th century, under the reign of Josiah (640-609) if not of Manasseh (697-642). But Elephantine is rather an exception than the rule. On the whole, historical reality has a somber hue.

The Alexandrian translators refused to face this reality. In their presentation of the *golah* as a "colony" (*apoikia* or *apoikesia*), they retrospectively aligned the Jewish past with the Greek past. The circumstances of the times may have justified this "revisionism." Since Alexander's conquests, Jews had been allowed to participate in the new Greek colonial enterprise. They constituted an integral part of the dominant community of Greek speaking immigrants. As Philo put it (*In Flaccum* 46), they held the Holy City to be their "mother city," *metropolis*, while the new Greek cities where they were living are in each case accounted by them to be their "fatherland," *patrides*; to some of them, as Alexandria or Antioch, they have come at the time of their foundation as "colonists" (ἀποικίαν στειλάμενοι) to the satisfaction of the founders. The Jew's perception of his own history bears the mark of the Greek example. The present dictates the interpretation of the past.

But there is also a future, and, here again, the paths of the two peoples diverge. Among the Greeks, no one awaited or desired the colonists' return to their starting point – the cities and the regions of ancient Greece which had furnished the human material for Alexander's conquest of the East. The Jews believed, on the contrary, that they would one day return to the land their God had given them. The Lord would seek them out even in "the outmost parts of heaven," gather them together and lead them back to the land of their fathers (Dt 30, 4-5; cf. 2M 1, 27). This is indubitably the end of a *dispersion,* and not the repatriation of a colony. In order to express this eschatological perspective, the semantic field of a word group had been modified: *diaspora, diaspeirein* and their derivatives, heretofore narrowly specific, took on a new meaning.[13]

Unless and until further detailed research alters our conclusions, the modern idea of diaspora appears to be an invention of Alexandrian Judaism. The following chapters are due to Christian pens.[14] In the

---

[13]A "neologism": C. Dogniez & M. Harl, *La Bible d'Alexandrie, 5: Le Deutéronome,* Paris 1992, p. 289 (cf. p. 64).

[14]The sources are available in A. Stuiber, "Diaspora", in Reallexikon f. Antike u. Altertum, III, Stuttgart 1957, col. 972-982, esp. 975 ff.("Die jüdische D. in christlicher Beurteilung"). More recently, the posthumous work of W.C. van Unnik, *Das Selbstverständnis der jüdischen Diaspora in der hellenistisch-römischen Zeit,* ed. by P.W. van der Horst, Leiden 1993 (Arbeiten zur Geschichte des Antiken Judentums und des Urchristentums, 17), investigates the semantic field of the term *diaspora* in the Septuagint and in the New Testament as well as in post-biblical Jewish and Christian writings.

Gospels (John 7, 35; probably also the *Epistle of James* 1, 1) and the *Acts of the Apostles* (8,4), the terms *diaspora* and *diaspeirō* refer simply to Jews living among Greeks. After the destruction of the Second Temple in 70 CE the Fathers of the Church stressed the repressive aspect of the scattering of the Jewish people throughout the world; they saw it as a just retribution for the crime of which the Jews are held guilty since, as Origen put it, "they contrived a plot against the Savior of the human race" (*C. Celsum* 5, 22).

Mutatis mutandis, the Christian way of looking at things matches the viewpoint of the Rabbis, for whom the catastrophes visited upon the Jews are mostly interpreted as the punishment of Heaven for the sins they have committed. The only significant difference lies in the nature of the criminal act, not in the logic of this metaphysical causality. From this confluence a parallel has been drawn between the misfortunes of the *galuth* and the dispersion of the Jews, "driven from their land by the vicissitudes of their history."

However, dispersion is not always – and should not be – synonymous with "affliction." Another opinion, represented by a few Sages, interprets the dispersion of the Jews as a divine intervention furthering their proselytic mission (*lekarev et hagerim*). As early as the beginning of the third century CE, a Palestinian amora, Hoshaiah Rabbah, expressed the view that "the dispersion was a blessing for Israel" (*b. Pes.* 87b). For R. Eleazar ben Pedath, another Palestinian amora of the end of the third century CE, "[God] did not exile Israel among the nations save in order that proselytes might join them, for it is said: 'I will sow her unto me in the land' [Ho 2, 25]."[15] The Hebrew text of Hosea to which R. Eleazar is referring plays on words by juxtaposing *Yizre'el* (2, 24) and *uzera^Ctiha* ("I will sow," 2, 25). In the Greek version of this text (LXX Ho 2, 25) *uzera^Ctiha* becomes *sperō* (σπερῶ), the future tense of *speirō* (σπείρω), a verb from which *diaspora* is derived. R. Eleazar obviously knew the Greek etymology of "dispersion." The positive evaluation of the "dispersion" by the Sages apparently originates in a Jewish rejoinder to the Christian interpretation of the notion of *diaspora*.

---

[15]Ibid. See M. Simon, *Verus Israel* (English version by H. McKeating), Oxford 1986, p. 275ff. (and p. 483, note 20). For the attribution to R. Eleazar ben Pedath, cf. E.E. Urbach, *The Sages. Their Concepts and Beliefs*, Jerusalem 1975, I, p. 542ff. W.C. van Unnik, *Das Selbstverständnis*, op. cit., p. 145f., would prefer Eleazar bar Qappara (c. 225 CE), possibly identifiable with the Jewish opponent of Origen in *C. Celsum* 1, 55.

II. – Jewish diaspora, Greek colonialism

The origin and meaning of the word *diaspora* in ancient days has aroused our curiosity and brought us to Jewish circles in Alexandria, a particular variation on the general theme of this conference: a new Jewish diaspora as an integral part of what could be called a new Greek diaspora, which was actually a new political structure of a colonial type. The situation, fraught with consequences for the future, was as new for the Jews as it was for the Greeks.[16]

Up to the end of the fourth century BCE, Jews and Greeks hardly knew each other. Their paths had led them in various directions, affording few opportunites for meeting. The "Deuteronomic Historian" informs us that King David had Cretan soldiers among his personal guards (2S 8, 18). At that epoch, about 1000 BCE, they would have spoken an archaic Dorian dialect. Four centuries later, other Greek soldiers, also speaking a Dorian dialect, could possibly have encountered members of the Judean garrison of Elephantine, in Egypt. It seems that Jewish troops indeed took part in the Nubian campaign of King Psammetichus II in 593 BCE, along with Rhodian mercenaries, who scribbled graffiti on the foot of one of the four colossal statues adorning Ramses II's stone temple in Abu-Simbel.[17] But let us not labor under an illusion: one cannot demand of David's Cretans and Psammetichus' Rhodians the opening of a dialogue of consequence between Greeks and Jews.

Greek sources for that period are rare; all in all, we possess only two literary texts possibly concerning the Jews. Both are indirect references. The first is a note by Herodotus (2, 104) about the practice of circumcision by the "Syrians in Palestine,"[18] whom Josephus (*Ant.* 8, 262; *C. Apion.* 1, 168 sq.) has, perhaps properly, identified as Jews. Herodotus

---

[16]To the bibliography quoted in my book, *Juifs d'Égypte*, p. 197ff., add M. Stern, Ed., *The Diaspora in the Hellenistic and Roman World*, Jerusalem 1983 (Hebrew), with a chapter on "Jews in Egypt" by U. Rappaport, p. 21-53; W.D. Davies & L. Finkelstein, Eds., *The Cambridge History of Judaism*, II, Cambridge 1989, with a chapter on "The Diaspora in the Hellenistic age" by H. Hagermann, p. 115-166. See also R.J Coggins, "The origins of the Jewish diaspora", in R.E. Clements, Ed. *The World of Ancient Israel*, Cambridge 1989, p. 163-181; J.A. Overman & R.S. MacLennan, Eds., *Diaspora Jews and Judaism. Essays in Honor of, and in Dialogue with, A. Thomas Kraabel*, University of South Florida 1992, including several pioneering studies on the Greco-Roman diaspora. An international colloquium on "The Jewish Diaspora in the Hellenistic and Roman Periods" was organized in Tel Aviv in January 1991 by the Chaim Rosenberg School of Jewish Studies, Tel Aviv University; as far as I know, its proceedings have not yet been published.

[17]A. Bernand & O. Masson, "Les inscriptions grecques d'Abou-Simbel", Rev. des études grecques 70, 1957, p. 1-20. See my *Juifs d'Égypte*, p. 22ff.

[18]Reinach no. l; Stern no. l.

was thus aware of a practice one could attribute to the Jews, rather than of the Jews themselves. The second text is a Greek papyrus from Egypt, P. Oxy. XLI 2944, which shows that biblical scenes out of context, in the present case the celebrated judgment of Solomon (IR 3, 16-28), were known in Athens before the beginning of Alexander's Eastern campaigns. The authorship of the judgment in question gave rise to a dispute among the Greeks. However neither Solomon nor the Jews are mentioned in the papyrus as it has come down to us.[19] It was not until the end of the fourth century, in 315-314 BCE, that the term *Ioudaioi* appeared in a text of Theophrastus quoted by Porphyry (*De abst.* 2, 26, *ap.* Eusebius, *Praep. ev.* 9, 2): this is the first time Jews are mentioned in Greek sources.[20]

Things were a bit better on the Jewish side. Several biblical texts speak of Yavan, at one and the same time a region, an ethnic group and an individual representing that group. He appears as early as the seventh century BCE in the "Table of Nations" (Gn 10, 2 & 4) as the son of Japheth who, in turn, is the father of four sons; the youngest of these, Rodanim, is an early presage of the Rhodians of Abu-Simbel. Yavan is a rather unsympathetic character, involved in shady deals with partners in Asia Minor (Ez 27, 12-13) and with the Philistines, who sell him the children of Judea and Jerusalem (Jl 4, 4-6). He winds up as the personification of Israel's enemies (Zc 9, 13). The Jews, then, knew the Greeks better than the Greeks the Jews. But this knowledge is partial and bears a negative sign. Until the time of Alexander, the Jewish image of the Greek is that of a slave merchant with whom one would rather not be seen.

When Alexander made his appearance, everything changed. The paths of the Greeks and the Jews had crossed at last. And the Jews found themselves in the Greek sphere of influence. The image of the slave merchant disappeared. In its stead, there arose the figure of a powerful King, protector of the Holy City of Jerusalem, guardian of the Torah as the "ancestral law" of the Jews. Josephus (*Ant.* 11, 326-339) records the dramatic encounter of Alexander and the high priest Jaddus in Jerusalem. Whether or not this now legendary piece of writing can be taken at its face value and whatever its origin, Alexandrian or Palestinian, it can stand on its own as a political platform.[21] The Jews

---

[19]On this text, see my study "Philiscos de Milet et le jugement de Salomon: la première référence grecque à la Bible", Bull. Ist. Dir. Rom. 91 (3 ser. 30), 1988 [publ. 1992], p. 571-597.

[20]Reinach no. 5; Stern no. 4.

[21]Shaye J.D. Cohen, "Alexander the Great and Jaddus the High Priest according to Josephus", Assoc. for Jewish Studies Review 7/8 (1982/83), 1987, p. 41-68.

agreed to serve the Hellenistic sovereign, who promised in turn to respect their national and cultural identity. This policy applies to Judea and the Jews living in Babylonia as well as to the new Western diaspora soon to arise in Alexandria and on the shores of the Nile. The Jews joined forces with the Greeks in what is later to be called "the Hellenization of the East."

The second great Hellenic colonization did not resemble the first, in which the Greeks generally followed the Mediterranean coastline and the shores of the Black Sea. The "new Hellenization" went right to the heart of the territories conquered "at spearpoint" (δορύκτητος). New towns, were established and urban concentrations arose within the Egyptian "metropoleis," once large villages but now swollen with the influx of new immigrants. The conquered countryside served and fed the Greek towns, which dominated it. The conquest compounded the ancient antagonism between city and countryside, proper to the Greek mainland, and the external antagonism between Greeks and barbarians. Monopoly of power fell into the hands of the Greco-Macedonian conquerors, whose representatives were chosen among the dynasties founded by Alexander's generals and the Hellenistic "herrschende Gesellschaft" that paid court to them.[22] "Colonization" is a more appropriate term for this new Greek expansion than for the older one of the archaic era.

Let us beware of anachronisms. Comparison with present day colonial systems may prove misleading.[23] The undeniable social and economic inequalities that the conquerors imposed on the conquered do not necessarily imply the practice of juridical discrimination or a kind of "apartheid." The Macedonian conquest did not turn the Easterners into "Greek helots," as Isocrates would have had it.[24] Thus, in Ptolemaic Egypt, actual inequalities went hand-in-hand with the formal equality of immigrants and "natives." Although the system of property rights favored the Greco-Macedonian colonist, the cleruch, to the detriment of the indigenous peasant, careers in the royal administration were equally

---

[22]This question has been dealt with by L. Mooren in his studies quoted in Stud. Doc. Hist. Iur. 47, 1981, p. 541-542 (Arch. f. Pap. 32, 1986, p. 101). See his paper "Macht und Nationalität", in *Das ptolemäische Ägypten,* Mainz 1978, p. 51-57.
[23]Éd. Will, "Pour une 'anthropologie coloniale' du monde hellénistique", in *Essays in honor of Ch.G. Starr,* New York & London 1985, p. 273-301. See B. Anagnostou-Canas, "Rapports de dépendance coloniale dans l'Égypte ptolémaïque, I. L'appareil militaire," Bull. Ist. Dir. Rom. 92-93 (3 ser. 32-33), 1989-1990 [publ. 1993], p. 151-236; "II. Les rebelles de la chora", in Proc. XIXth Intern. Congr. of Papyrology, Cairo 1992, II, p. 323-372; "III. La colonisation du sol dans l'Égypte ptolémaïque", in *Grund und Boden im Altägypten,* proceedings of an international conference held in Tübingen in June 1990 (forthcoming).
[24]Isocrates, *Letter to Philip,* 5.

open to all comers, provided they knew Greek, the tongue of the dominant group. Key posts, especially in the royal chancellery and the army's high command, were always assigned to Greek immigrants.[25] But one could conceive of the dialogue between royal government and the high clergy of Memphis as a kind of "bicephalous monarchy" under the Egyptian reign of Ptolemy II Philadelphus.[26] This sovereign instituted a judicial system which treated the laws and customs of the two populations on a strictly egalitarian basis.[27]

It would, in any case, be misguided to blame the Jews for their participation in an enterprise of "colonial exploitation." Like the Greeks, the Macedonians, the Thracians and Galatians, and so many others, they did not travel to Egypt to alleviate the sufferings of the native peasants. The image of Egyptian Jewry as a "hard-working people earning its living by tenacious labor"[28] is not a realistic one. Egypt attracted the Jews, as it attracted other immigrants, by the possibilities it offered of making one's fortune. In a state established by military conquest, the conquerors were, first and foremost, soldiers. The typical Egyptian Jew was the cleruch, a military colonist whose services were rewarded by the granting of a plot of land (*klēros*).

The *Letter of Aristeas* (§ 12-14), followed by Josephus (*Ant.* 12, 12-33), informs us that Ptolemy I deported 100 000 Jews from Judea to Egypt. This information is linked to the tradition, conserved by Agatharchides of Cnidus and reproduced by Josephus (*C. Apion.* 1, 208-211; *Ant.* 12, 5-6), according to which Ptolemy I took Jewish captives with him into Egypt. Papyrological evidence which was supposed to corroborate this information does not confirm its historicity.[29] Our knowledge of the first Jewish settlements in Egypt favors the opposing tradition, attributed to Hecataeus of Abdera, according to which the Jews followed the king

---

[25]See the studies of the late W. Peremans: "Égyptiens et étrangers dans l'administration civile et financière de l'Égypte ptolémaïque", Anc. Soc. 2, 1971, p. 33-45; "Égyptiens et étrangers dans l'armée de terre et dans la police de l'Égypte ptolémaïque", ibid. 3, 1972, p. 67-76; "Égyptiens et étrangers dans le clergé, le notariat et les tribunaux de l'Égypte ptolémaïque", ibid. 4, 1973, p. 59-69.

[26]W. Peremans, "Les Lagides, les élites indigènes et la monarchie bicéphale", in É. Lévy, Ed., *Le système palatial en Orient, en Grèce et à Rome.* Actes du Colloque de Strasbourg, juin 1985, Leiden 1987, p. 327-343.

[27]See my art. "Droit et justice dans le monde hellénistique au IIIe siècle avant notre ère. Expérience lagide", in *Mnêmê G. A. Petropoulou*, Athens 1984, I, p. 53-77.

[28]V. Tcherikover, *Prolegomena*, p. 19.

[29]The principal document concerning this problem is a *prostagma* of Ptolemy II Philadelphus dated 260 BCE, PER 24552 = C.Ord.Ptol. 21-22. See the discussion in I. Biezunska-Malowist, *L'esclavage dans l'Égypte gréco-romaine, I. Période ptolémaïque*, Wroclaw 1974, p. 19ff.

voluntarily (*ap*. Josephus, C. *Apion*. 1, 183-204).[30] Although the existence of Jewish captives in third century Egypt remains a plausible hypothesis in individual cases, massive deportations and freeing of slaves were hardly compatible with the policy of the first Ptolemies in this matter.[31] Voluntary immigration was by far the principal source of the Jewish establishment in the Ptolemaic kingdom. In this respect, the Jewish diaspora in Egypt was a *tefuṣah* rather than a *golah*. Let us consider the situation from this point of view.

The Greeks who came to Egypt after the Macedonian conquest retained their original mainland citizenship. Some of them acquired new citizenship in the cities founded by Alexander and Ptolemy I, Alexandria and Ptolemais. However a good many of these immigrants were not city-dwellers, but lived in the countryside, or, to be more precise, in the large provincial towns which, despite their urban appearance and names (often using the term polis), did not formally have the official status of a city.[32] An Athenian who had settled in Crocodilopolis, in the Fayûm, did not become a "Crocodilopolitan" (*Krokodilopolitēs* in Greek). He remained an *Athēnaios*, as did his descendants, since citizenship was hereditary.[33] As the generations went by, the bonds which united the immigrants to their ancestral homelands became looser and looser. The great-grandson of our *Athēnaios* was no more Athenian than an American Kennedy is Irish, or a Vanderbilt Dutch. It would be difficult for a "true" Athenian to recognize him as a fellow citizen. But in Egypt, this reference to a civic homeland was a vital matter for the immigrants' descendants: it guaranteed their belonging to the community of Hellenes, a novel manner of being Greek in foreign territory.[34]

The Greeks had always been acutely aware of their cultural and ethnic unity, of having "one and the same blood" (ὅμαιμον), "one and the same tongue" (ὁμόγλωσσον), the same cults (θεῶν ἱδρύματά τε κοινὰ καὶ θυσίαι) and customs (ἤθεά τε ὁμότροπα), as Herodotus put it in a well-remembered formula (8, 44). The community of worship and of custom

---

[30]Stern no. 12.

[31]Sic I. Biezunska-Malowist, *L'esclavage*, op. cit., p. 23ff. In this respect, the position of E.L. Abel, "The Myth of Jewish Slavery in Ptolemaic Egypt," Rev. ét. juives – Historia Iudaica 127, 1968, p. 253-258, is still creditworthy against the tendencies of modern research.

[32]See H. Cadell, "Pour une recherche sur *astu* et *polis* dans les papyrus grecs d'Égypte", Ktema 9, 1984, p. 235-246.

[33]See A. Martin, "Ἀθήναιοι et ' Ἀθηναῖοι en Égypte gréco-romaine", Anc. Soc. 20, 1989, p. 169-184, and my remarks in Journ. Jur. Pap. 22, 1992, p. 183.

[34]See my art. "Le statut des Hellènes dans l'Égypte lagide. Bilan et perspectives de recherches", Rev. des études grecques 96, p. 241-268 (= *Statut personnel et liens de famille dans les droits de l'Antiquité*, Aldershot 1993, n° III).

bound them together, notwithstanding their political division. The Hellenistic monarchy of Egypt raised this unity to the level of an institutional category. Although they did not follow Isocrates' prescription in their treatment of conquered foreigners, the Ptolemies fulfilled his desire "that the name of Hellene be not that of a particular ethnic group, but rather of a way of thinking, and that one should call Hellenes those who have shared our education and not those who share our origin" (*Paneg.*, 50).

As a matter of fact, the status of "Hellene" was recognized as rightfully belonging not only to immigrants from an authentic city-state or federation of city-states, such as Athens or Crete, but also to a mass of individuals stemming from the North and Northwest regions who had never lived in cities, as well as those from lands once considered as barbarian but which were now included in the expanding cultural sphere of the Grecian universe. Thrace fell into this category, as did, of course, Macedonia, motherland of the royal family and of a good part of the Ptolemaic elite. By extension, Asiatics and Semites from the countries Alexander had conquered were also to be considered "Hellenes," provided they spoke Greek and served the royal dynasty. New solidarities were born, the fruit of neighborliness consolidated by the comradeship of arms, in juxtaposition with the particularities of various national traditions, within the new community of "Hellenes" which guaranteed to each of its members a status reconciling the maintenance of his own national identity with his incorporation into the dominant group. This state of affairs suited the Jews perfectly.

A considerable part of the Jewish population lived in Alexandria; traditionally, this settlement is supposed to have begun during Alexander's lifetime. However, like so many other inhabitants of that great cosmopolitan city, the Jews, barring a few exceptional cases, were not, properly speaking, Alexandrian citizens. According to the author of the *Letter of Aristeas* (§ 310) they had their "elders," *presbyteroi* (πρεσβύτεροι), and their "leaders" (ἡγούμενοι τοῦ πλήθους). At the end of the Ptolemaic period and at the beginning of the Roman domination an ethnarch administered Jewish affairs in Alexandria "like the head of an autonomous civic community" (Strabo *ap.* Josephus, *Ant.* 14, 117.)[35] However, this does not signify that Alexandrian Jews formed a "civic

---

[35]The powers of the ethnarch should not be overestimated, as they are by Tcherikover, *Prolegomena*, p. 10. Thus, in the judicial domain, e.g., they are limited to a kind of arbitration: see H.J. Wolff, *Das Justizwesen der Ptolemäer*, München 1962 (2nd ed. 1971), p. 21, and my art. "Zum Justizwesen der Ptolemäer", Ztschr. Sav.-Stift., Rom. Abt. 80, 1963, p. 42-82, esp. 50ff. On Strabo's text, C. Préaux, "Les étrangers à l'époque hellénistique", in Rec. Soc. J. Bodin, 9: L'Étranger, 1. L'Antiquité, Brussels 1958, p. 141-193, esp. 166ff.

community" called *politeuma*, a term which appears only, as far as they are concerned, in the above quoted passage of *Letter of Aristeas*, and to which some modern scholars have given more importance than it deserves.[36] Since they were not "Alexandrians" (*Alexandreis*), they were "Jews of Alexandria" (*Ioudaioi hoi apo Alexandreias*, 'Ιουδαῖοι οἱ ἀπὸ 'Αλεξανδρείας): this is the term a certain Helenos, son of Tryphon, used to identify himself, when the rank of citizen he claimed to have directly inherited from his father had been put into question.[37]

In this respect, the Jewish settlement in Alexandria did not differ from those we encounter in the *chōra*: Jews of this or that town (*apo*) or residing in such and such a place (*en*). This applies to "the Jews of Xenephyris" (οἱ ἀπὸ Ξενεφύρεως 'Ιουδαῖοι; CPJud. III App. I, 1441); "the Jews living in Nitriai" (οἱ ἐν Νιτρίαις 'Ιουδαῖοι; ibid. 1442); "in Athribis" (οἱ ἐν 'Ατρίβει 'Ιουδαῖοι; ibid. 1443) or "in Crocodilopolis" (οἱ ἐν Κροκοδίλων πόλει 'Ιουδαῖοι; ibid. 1532A). These groups provide an excellent illustration of one meaning of the term *Ioudaios* that Shaye Cohen has so clearly brought to light: a member of the Jewish nation living in the diaspora.[38]

The Jews in the Egyptian *chora* also had their representatives, called *presbyteroi* (πρεοβύτεροι), the "elders," or even *archontes* (ἄρχοντες), the "rulers," terms which are well known from literary and epigraphical sources outside Egypt. A recently published papyrus from the second century BCE (P.Monac. III 49) mentions Jewish *presbyteroi* in Tebetnoi and Jewish *archontes* in Herakleopolis. *Archontes* may here designate the heads of the local synagogue. This is the meaning of this term in the only

---

[36]So especially A. Kasher, *The Jews in Hellenistic and Roman Egypt*, Tel-Aviv 1978 (Hebrew), and Tübingen 1985 (English). My critical remarks on his theories, Rev. hist. droit 58, 1980, p. 514ff. (Stud. Doc. Hist. Iur. 49, 1983, p. 665; Arch. f. Pap. 33, 1987, p. 128), are shared by C. Zuckerman, "Hellenistic politeumata and the Jews. A Reconsideration", Scripta Class. Israel. 8-9 (1985-1988), 1989, p. 171-185, and confirmed, as far as the notion of *politeuma* is concerned, by D.J. Thompson Crawford, "The Idumaeans of Memphis and the Ptolemaic Politeumata", in Atti XVII Congr. intern. di Papirologia, Naples 1984, p. 1069-1075. On Kasher's book see also Shaye J.D. Cohen, "Kasher's Jews in Egypt", Jew. Quart. Rev. 72, No. 4, 1982, p. 330-331. Kasher's thesis is resumed in his articles "Diaspora, I/2. Frühjüdische und rabbinische Zeit", Theol. Realenzykl. VIII, 4.5, Berlin & New York 1985, p. 711-717 and more recently "The Civic Status of the Jews in Ptolemaic Egypt", in P. Bilde, & others, Eds., *Ethnicity in Hellenistic Egypt*, Aarhus 1992, p. 100-121.

[37]CPJud. II 151. See my *Juifs d'Égypte*, p. 133ff., and D. Delia, *Alexandrian Citizenship During the Roman Principate*, Atlanta, Georgia, 1991, p. 26f.

[38]Shaye J.D. Cohen, "Religion, Ethnicity, and 'Hellenism' in the Emergence of Jewish Identity in Maccabean Palestine", in P. Bilde, & others, Ed., *Religion and Religious Practice in the Seleucid Kingdom*, Aarhus 1990, p. 205.

other document in which it formerly appeared (CPJud. II 432).[39] On the other hand, no mention of a Jewish *politeuma* in the *chora* occurs in Ptolemaic documents. The reference to *politikoi nomoi* ("civic laws") in the royal *diagramma* presented by a Jewish litigant to the local court in Crocodilopolis (CPJud. I 19) is not sufficient evidence for the existence of a Jewish *politeuma* in this town[40]: the *diagramma* was not issued for the Jews alone, but for all Greek speaking immigrants.[41] The same applies to the poetical use of the terms *politai*, "fellow citizens" (CPJud. III App. I, 1489), and *politarchēs*, "ruler of a city" (CPJud. III App. I, 1530 A), in the epigraphical material from the necropolis of Tel el-Yehoudieh; these texts can hardly support the supposition that the Jewish settlement in Leontopolis was "organized as a *politeuma*."[42] The idea that "the measure of autonomy" enjoyed by such purely imaginary *politeumata* "could easily stand comparison with that accorded to Greek cities at the time" is totally unwarranted.[43]

If the Jews in Ptolemaic Egypt enjoyed a kind of "civic status," it is not because they were organized in "civic communities;" the deciding factor is that they belonged to the community of Hellenes which was "civic" as opposed to the native population. From the Greek viewpoint, the ethnic designation *Ioudaios* opened the portals of this community to the Jews, as other "foreign" ethnics did; all those who adhered to Greek culture by adopting its tongue and its social customs, and who could give proof of a respectable origin outside Egypt, were regarded as "Greek." In the third century BCE, in Trikômia (Fayûm), a village having a considerable Jewish population, a number of persons most of whom, if not all, were Jewish, were listed as "Hellenes living in the house of Marôn" (CPR XIII 4, col. VII, 109).[44] We can draw a parallel between

---

[39]On this whole question, see the commentary of the editor, D. Hagedorn, p. 9ff.

[40]Sic A. Kasher, in P. Bilde, & others, Eds., *Ethnicity in Hellenistic Egypt* (above, note 36), p. 108.

[41]On *politikoi nomoi*, see my study "La règle de droit dans l'Égypte ptolémaïque. État des questions et perspectives de recherches", in *Essays in honor of C. Bradford Welles* (American Studies of Papyrology, vol. 1), New Haven 1966, p. 125-173; cf. my art. "Droit et justice, etc.", quoted above, note 27. On the Septuagint as a *politikos nomos* for Egyptian Jews, see below, note 47.

[42]A. Kasher, l.c., p. 108-109. The reference to Strabo speaking of *politai* (*ap.* Josephus, *Ant.* 13, 287) and *politeia* in connection with Jews in Leontopolis and in Alexandria (*ibid.* 14, 117; cf. above, note 35) is not pertinent. What Strabo has in mind is the fact of belonging to the Jewish people, and not citizenship *sensu stricto*.

[43]H. Hagermann, *The Cambridge History of Judaism*, II, 1989 (above, note 16), p. 160.

[44]The problem has been examined by W. Clarysse in his paper "A Jewish community in Trikomia" presented to the 20th International Congress of

this document and the complaint of the Macedonian Ptolemaios, son of Glaukias, concerning an outrage perpetrated against him "although he was a Hellene" (παρὰ τὸ "Ελληνά με εἶναι).[45] We see that to be a *Ioudaios* in Ptolemaic Egypt is not very different from being a *Makedōn*. Facing the native Egyptians, both are "Hellenes."

The emergence of a self-definition for the Jews in Ptolemaic Egypt under the influence of the Septuagint did not change this situation.[46] Neither "citizens" nor "autonomous aliens," the Jews are one of the various elements composing the society of Greek speaking conquerors. Nothing but his religion distinguishes a Jew from his Greco-Macedonian neighbors. He is a full-fledged member of the dominant group of "Hellenes," the equal of any other Greek speaking immigrant. The problem now arises: how to be a Jew and a Greek at one and the same time?

III. – The limits of allegiance

As a general rule, membership in the Hellenic community was compatible with fidelity to Judaism. Language presented no problem. The use of Greek, even in synagogal practice, was not considered a transgression. The Sages of the Talmud deemed the Greek translation of the Torah to be a perfectly legitimate enterprise, and even an inspired one, notwithstanding the errors committed by the translators (*b. Megillah* 8b-9b). Rabbi Shimon ben Gamliel, that admirer of Greek wisdom, went so far as to proclaim the uniquely privileged character of the Greek language, the only "other tongue" authorized by Scripture (*ibid.*). To justify this opinion, the Talmud invokes the "beauty of Japhet" (Gn 9, 27), appreciated by the Jews, in contrast to their poor opinion of Japheth's son, Yavan. The opposite position holds square Hebrew characters (*ktav ashuri*) to be the only possible written vehicle for Scripture and likens the day when the Torah was translated into Greek for King Ptolemy to the day when the ancient Israelites fashioned the Golden Calf (*Massekhet Soferim*, 1,7). This stand should be placed in its historical context, as it embodies reservations concerning the Septuagint, a translation made by Jews for Jews, but later transformed into the Christian Bible after the destruction of Alexandrian Judaism in the wake of the revolt of 115-117 CE.

Papyrology (Copenhagen, August 1992; forthcoming in the Proceedings of the Congress).

[45]P. Par. 36 = UPZ I 7, 13-14, and P. Lond. I 44 (p. 33) = UPZ I 8, 14 (163/161 BCE).

[46]See the contribution of Sylvie Honigman to this volume: "The Birth of a Diaspora : The Emergence of a Jewish Self-Definition in Ptolemaic Egypt in the Light of Onomastics".

What the talmudic texts do not tell us is the position the Septuagint was supposed to occupy in the Ptolemaic judicial system, as the body of "civil law," *politikos nomos*, for the Jews of Egypt. The papyrological evidence, especially the parallel that may be drawn between the Greek translation of Jewish Law and the translation of the demotic Law-Book, throws new light on this point of contention, seriously modifying the opposing positions in the debate on the origins and purpose of the "Alexandrian Bible."[47] In actual daily practice, the Jews of Egypt appear to stray from the observance of their national law in favor of Greek law; this fact poses another problem, to be considered in the pluralistic context of Jewish law during the Second Commonwealth. In any event, liberties taken with the law of *ribbit* or with the biblical rules governing divorce do not amount to "apostasy."[48]

In contrast to the Roman army, full of heathen symbolism, the Ptolemaic army held no danger for Jewish religious integrity. Thus, many Jews were able to make brilliant careers in Egypt. We are not obliged to take Josephus literally when he claims that Ptolemy VI Philometor and his wife Cleopatra II "entrusted their entire kingdom to the Jews and put two Jews at the head of their army, Onias and Dositheus, whose names Apion mocked" (*C. Apion*, 2, 49). But one can readily trust the documents in which Jewish officers are mentioned.

Thus we learn, in an inscription from the second or first century BCE, how a police officer, Ptolemaios, son of Epikydes, almost certainly a Jew, joined forces with the Jews of Athribis to help found a synagogue (CPJud. III, App. I, 1443). At Thebes in Upper Egypt, in 158 BCE, we come across one Iasibis, a cavalry officer (epistates of hipparchy), who took part in the sale of a house which had been confiscated by the royal treasury (CPJud. I 27). The editors of CPJud. are probably right in asssuming that this name is one of the Greek variants of the Hebrew *Yashib* or *Yashub*, which the Septuagint renders by *Iasoub, Iasoubos, Iasseib* or *Iassēb*, the hypocoristic form of the theophoric name *Eliyashib* or

---

[47]See my art. "'Livres sacrés' et justice lagide", in J. Kodrebski, Ed., *Symbolae C. Kunderewicz oblatae* (Acta Universitatis Lodziensis, Folia Juridica 21), Lodz 1986, p. 11-44. Cf. *Juifs d'Égypte*, p. 84ff. I have again dealt with this problem in a paper entitled "How did the Torah become a 'civic law' for the Jews in Ptolemaic Egypt?", presented to the Seventh Biennial Conference of the Jewish Law Association, Paris, July 1992 (forthcoming in Israel Law Review, Special Issue in honor of R. Yaron).

[48]On the law of *ribbit* in the practice of the Jews in Egypt, see my *Juifs d'Égypte*, p. 94ff. On divorce, see my art. "Les Juifs et le droit hellénistique: divorce et égalité des époux (CPJud. 144)", Iura 12, 1961, p. 162-193. New evidence: CPR XVIII 9 (Samaria, 232 BCE); see my remarks Journ. Jur. Pap. 22, 1992, p. 290.

Yehoyashib. The hypothesis of a Jewish officer under the reign of the "philosemitic" King Ptolemy VI is entirely plausible.

We do not know how the Jewish soldiers of the Ptolemaic kings managed to reconcile their military obligations with the Sabbath rest, whose respect is attested by the papyri (CPJud. I 106; PSI XVII Congr. 22, 25). A few mutual concessions were probably enough to surmount all difficulties. That the Ptolemaic monarchy extended its protection to cover Jewish religious practice is clearly shown by the dedications of synagogues in honor of the sovereign (ὑπὲρ βασιλέως) and his family, from the middle of the third century (CPJud. III, App. I, 1440 & 1532 A) onwards. They are, on the one hand, proof of loyalty on the Jews' part, and on the other, formal testimony of the acceptance by the royal power of the Jewish communities' initiative, implying official protection of synagogical worship. The king may go further yet, by granting a synagogue the privilege of the right of asylum, as he did for the pagan temples. The document recording this act (CPJud. III App. I, 1449), which was for a long time ascribed to Queen Zenobia of Palmyra, actually dates from the reign of the last Cleopatra.[49]

The episode of the temple of Leontopolis has a similar context.[50] Josephus quotes the correspondence between Onias IV and Ptolemy VI Philometor and his sister-wife Cleopatra II (*Ant.* 13, 64-71) concerning the project of erecting a Jewish temple on the ruins of a fortress once dedicated to the Egyptian cat goddess Bastet-the-Wild, on a site where sacred animals abounded. The royal pair, whose approval was necessary, approached the project with circumspection. The King and Queen proved to be more scrupulous in their concern for the purity of the Jewish cult than the Jewish high priest himself, who had taken refuge in Egypt. Ptolemy VI, whose sympathy for the Jews was well-known, was not but could very well have been one of the sovereigns whom Josephus promoted to the rank of "adherent" or "convert" to Judaism[51]. The correspondence in question is of doubtful authenticity, but the temple was actually built, and its site, as indicated by Josephus, has been confirmed by funerary epigraphy. As in the case of the synagogues, this implies understanding and cooperation between the monarchy and the Jews. The Sages of the Talmud seem to have approved these ties,

---

[49]J. Bingen, "L'asylie pour une synagogue (CIL Suppl. 6583 = CIJ 1449)", in *Studia P. Naster oblata*, II, Louvain 1982, p. 11-16 (= *Pages d'épigraphie grecque. Attique–Égypte [1952-1982]*, Brussels 1991, p. 45-50).

[50]See my *Juifs d'Égypte*, p. 101ff. Cf. A. Zivie, "Onias", Lexikon der Ägyptologie IV/4, Lief. 28, Wiesbaden 1981, col. 569-572.

[51]Shaye J.D. Cohen, "Respect for Judaism by Gentiles according to Josephus", Harv. Theol. Rev. 80 (4), 1987, p. 409-430.

judging – unlike Arnaldo Momigliano[52] – this sanctuary established in Egypt by a legitimate high priest to be in no way "schismatic," whatever intentions may have motivated the project at its origin.[53]

Thus, the inclusion of the Jewish diaspora within the Greek group did not inevitably lead to the compromising or destruction of Jewish identity either by assimilation or through the hostile action of the surrounding society, even if it aroused some criticism, whose traces we can follow in literary sources and papyri.[54] The only serious conflict we hear of can easily be explained, either as a tragic error of Ptolemy IV Philopator confusing the God of the Jews with Dionysus, if one adopts the viewpoint of the author of the *Third Book of Maccabees*[55], or as due to the particular situation engendered by the struggle among the children of Ptolemy V Ephiphanes, if one prefers, as does V. Tcherikover, Josephus' chronology (*C. Apion.* 2, 49-55).[56]

Only apostasy entails a break with Jewish identity. In those times, apostasy was synonymous with idolatry, the active worship of "other gods."[57] A famous example is known to us, that of Dositheus, son of Drimylus, a Jew by origin, who had "changed his customs and become estranged from his ancestral beliefs" (μεταβαλὼν τὰ νόμιμα καὶ τῶν πατρίων δογμάτων ἀπηλλοτριωμένος: 3M l, 3). Refuting the doubts of modern critics, who have challenged the historicity of this individual, a half-dozen Greek papyri and a demotic document all confirm it.[58] We first discover Dositheus between 240 and 224 BCE, when he held the office of *hypomnematographos*, the grand registrar of King Ptolemy III Euergetes I (CPJud. I 127 a-b). He accompanied the sovereign in his tour of the Fayûm (CPJud. I 127 c). He may also, and at the same time, have been a shipowner.[59] In the twenty-fifth year of Ptolemy III, 223/222 BCE, Dositheus became the eponymous priest of Alexander and the deified

---

[52]A. Momigliano, *Alien Wisdom. The Limits of Hellenization*, Cambridge 1975, p. 118.

[53]For a discussion of this point, see my *Juifs d'Égypte*, p. 104ff.

[54]See my art. "Sur l'antisémitisme païen", in M. Olender, Ed., *Pour Léon Poliakov. Le racisme : mythes et sciences*, Brussels 1981, p. 411-439.

[55]E.g. my *Juifs d'Égypte*, p. 117ff.

[56]Tcherikover, *Prolegomena*, p. 22.

[57]For Talmudic sources I refer to the doctoral dissertation of Simon Körner, *Le statut du prosélyte et de l'apostat en droit hébraïque et en droit israélien*, Paris 1988.

[58]A. Fuks, "Dositheos Son of Drimylos. A Prosopographical Note", Journ. Jur. Pap. 7/8, 1954, p. 205-209 = M. Stern & M. Amit, Eds., *Social Conflict in Ancient Greece*, Jerusalem & Leiden 1984, p.307-311; CPJud. I, 127a-e, p.230-236.

[59]P. Ryl. IV 576, as interpreted by H. Hauben, "A Jewish Shipowner in the Third-Century Ptolemaic Egypt", Anc. Soc. 10, p. 167-170.

Ptolemies in Alexandria. Today we possess three documents, two Greek and one demotic, attesting this promotion.[60]

The eponymous priesthood in Hellenistic Egypt was a purely Greek office; no Egyptian name figures among the priests and priestesses who succeeded one another in Alexandria and Ptolemais.[61] A Hellenized Jew who had, in the course of his career, risen in the ranks of the king's service, could perfectly well aspire to this office. As far as the Greeks were concerned, there was no problem. From the Jewish point of view, however, there is a total incompatibility between fidelity to Judaism and the practice of a non-Jewish religion. The prophets of Israel, from Hosea and Amos onwards, held that even the worship of the true God in a fashion smacking of pagan ritual is equivalent to apostasy. Despite the basically political character of the Alexandrian priesthood, the breach is patent.[62] Divine worship of a human during his lifetime or after his death is not compatible with Judaism.

Dositheus was a "Hellene," because he was a *Ioudaios*. Was he still a *Ioudaios* once he had attained the summit of his career? His ethnic does not appear in the documents we quoted above. But this is entirely natural since we are dealing with a well-known individual, a "V.I.P." We know the birthplace of Zenon, son of Agreophon, a man made famous by a voluminous collection of documents called the "Zenon Archive." He is *Kaunios*, born in Caunus in Caria (Asia Minor). However, we do not know the origin of his "boss" Apollonius, the all-powerful minister whose lands he managed. He was probably a Greek from Caria, too, as were the men in his immediate entourage; in the numerous texts in which his name is mentioned, he is called "Apollonius the dioiketes."[63] The same applies to our man; he is "Dositheus the hypomnematographos," or simply Dositheus.

This does not mean that, on his own initiative, he could have repudiated his status as *Ioudaios*. Royal law forbade, under pain of death, any arbitrary change of name or of ethnic designation.[64] The king was empowered to grant him Alexandrian citizenship. Dositheus, *Alexandreus* by royal favor, could then pay little heed to his status as a

---

[60]CPJud. I 127 d-e; P. dem. Berl. 3096, p. 6-7. Cf. W. Clarysse, G. Van der Veken, S.P. Vleeming, *The Eponymous Priests of Ptolemaic Egypt*, Leiden 1983, p. 14.

[61]W. Peremans, "Égyptiens et étrangers dans le clergé, etc." (quoted above note 25), Anc. Soc. 4, 1973, p. 61.

[62]For other, less shocking, cases, see E.J. Bickerman, *The Jews in the Greek Age*, Cambridge, Mass., 1988, p. 252ff.

[63]The sources are listed in P.W. Pestman & others, *A Guide to the Zenon Archive*, Leiden 1981, p. 292-293 (12).

[64]BGU VI 1213 (IIId cent. BCE) 3. See my art. "Le statut des Hellènes" (above note 34) p. 244ff.

member of the Jewish people, *ethnos tōn Ioudaiōn.* Did he perhaps think it possible for him to remain a "Jew by birth," *Ioudaios to genos* (Ἰουδαῖος τὸ γένος), while holding high office in the priesthood of a non-Jewish religion? Although it was unacceptable from the Jewish standpoint, such a pattern of "dual allegiance" was not incompatible with Ptolemaic law, which considered the ethnic, Jewish or any other, as just one of the various elements in the personal status of a "Hellene."

For an Alexandrian Greek in the time of Ptolemy III and his son Philopator, Dositheus' career was a model of social success. For the Jewish or Christian reader of the *Third Book of Maccabees,* he is an exemplary renegade. His case seems to be an isolated one.[65] For us, its main interest lies in its furnishing a valuable illustration of the difficulty of being, at one and the same time, both a Jew and a Greek in Ptolemaic Alexandria.

IV. – An intellectual's illusions

The problems posed by "dual allegiance" need not necessarily be couched in the dramatic form of a breach of Jewish identity. They may also be of an intellectual order. It is common knowledge that thinkers and scholars unnecessarily complicate matters which, for the ordinary mortal, are simple and straightforward. Demetrius the chronographer offers us a curious example of this sort of complication.[66]

Demetrius was the first Jewish historian we know of who wrote in Greek. He lived during the reign of Ptolemy IV Philopator (222-205 BCE). The latter part of the third century BCE brought hard times to the Jews. The *Third Book of Maccabees,* as has been noted, places the first conflict

---

[65]Kineas, son of Dositheus, eponymous priest of Ptolemy VI and Cleopatra I in Ptolemais, in 172/71 BCE (W. Clarysse, G. Van der Veken, S.P. Vleeming, *The Eponymous Priests,* op. cit., p. 45), has nothing to do with our Dositheus. The supposition of J. IJsewijn, *De sacerdotibus sacerdotiisque Alexandri Magni et Lagidarum eponymis,* Brussels 1961 (repr. Milano 1971), p. 101, that he could be Jewish ("fortasse natione Iudaeus") is invalidated by the remarks of L. Robert concerning the proper name Kineas in his article "De Delphes à l'Oxus. Inscriptions grecques nouvelles de Bactriane", C.R. Acad. Inscr. et Belles-Lettres, 1968, p. 416-457, esp. 435ff. (= *Opera Minora Selecta,* V, Amsterdam 1989, p. 510-551, esp. 527ff.). As to Adaios, son of Gorgias, eponymous priest of Alexander and the deified Ptolemies in 202/201 BCE (W. Clarysse, etc., op. cit., p. 18), he appears in the CPJud. (I 22 = P. Tebt. III/1 820, l. 2) only because some *Ioudaioi* (l. 36) are mentioned in this document. Ἀδαῖος, a Macedonian name, should be distinguished from the Semitic Ἀδδαῖος. See on these two priests S. Honigman, *Les Orientaux en Égypte à l'époque hellénistique et romaine. Lexique onomastique et commentaire* (Mémoire de l'Académie des Inscriptions et Belles-Lettres), Jerusalem 1991, p. 112 and 118ff.
[66]For the following, see my *Juifs d'Égypte,* p. 55ff.

between royal power and the Jewish community in Philopator's reign; only by a last minute miracle were the Jews saved from extermination. Was Demetrius one of those who were spared? It is hard to say, not only because of doubts concerning the historicity and the dating of this event, but also because we are ignorant of everything concerning the man himself, aside from the period in which he lived. We only know that he wrote a work *On the Kings of Judea*, an ill-chosen title, since the fragments which have come down to us all deal with the period prior to the Israelite monarchy. However, this sort of title, much in vogue at the time, justified placing a history of the Jewish people on the bookshelves next to the works (lost to posterity) containing the history of the Hellenistic monarchs.

These six fragments of biblical history "translated and improved" by the Alexandrian Jew Demetrius are quite strange.[67] Demetrius is reputed to have been the first Jewish author to engage systematically in historical criticism.[68] All well and good. But there is more to the picture. The idea that the credibility of a people's history could best be guaranteed by its antiquity was very much in the air in those days. For Demetrius it was precisely the credibility of Jewish history, as recorded in the biblical writings, that was in question. Demetrius was involved in the contest of "intellectuals" playing the game of "the older the better." To win the race, it was obviously necessary to know one's starting point. This is where other difficulties arose.

If one began counting from the First Olympiad (776/75 BCE) one would soon be beaten by the Orientals: their pyramids and holy books are so ancient that they correspond to the Greek mythological epoch, before the beginning of history proper. Some Greeks rose to the challenge and tried to raise the stakes: they rationalized mythology in an effort to construct a scientific pre-history for their culture, which would place it at least on an equal footing with oriental antiquity. In the third century BCE, the anonymous author of the *Parian Chronicle* managed, by dint of acrobatical calculations, to date the reign of Cecrops, first – and legendary – king of Athens, in the beginning of the sixteenth century BCE.[69] A wasted effort. The Egyptian priests had no trouble proving that their history was older than that of the Greeks. If necessary, they would

---

[67]Text and commentary in C.R. Holladay, *Fragments from Hellenistic Jewish Authors, I: The Historians*, Chico, Calif., 1983, p. 51-91.
[68]Holladay, op. cit., p. 53. See E. Bickerman, "The Jewish Historian Demetrios", in *Christianity, Judaism and Other Greco-Roman Cults. Studies for Morton Smith*, ed. J. Neusner, III, Leiden 1975, p.72-84; amended version in *Studies in Jewish and Christian History*, II, Leiden 1980, p.347-358.
[69]IG XII 5, 444 = FGrH II B 239, A 1-2.

not balk at considering Homer or Thales as profoundly indebted to the wise men of Egypt. Berossus, a Babylonian priest who lived in the time of Antiochus I (281/80-262/61 BCE) and wrote in Greek, followed in their footsteps: since the antediluvian Oannes, half-man-half-fish, a Babylonian like the author, had instructed mankind in the arts and sciences, there was nothing left for the Greeks to invent.[70]

Since this game was obviously over before it could begin, the Greeks renounced competing on these terms. The superiority of their culture was not to be sought in its antiquity. They relegated the uncertainties of a too distant past to the unverifiable domain of myth. "I write what appears to me to be true," declares Hecataeus of Miletus, ca. 500 BCE; and he adds, "the fables the Greeks exchange among themselves are nothing but fancies."[71] Now it so happens that the earliest history of the Jewish people would seem quite mythological from the Greek point of view. Demetrius, culturally Greek but Jewish at heart, was faced with a dilemma. Unlike his Greek intellectual guides, he was not free to detach the smallest item of Jewish history from its parent body. As an Alexandrian scholar and man of letters, he should have consigned a large part of this history to some mythological closet. As a Jew, he had to accept it in its entirety: there is no place for mythology in the Torah! Moreover, how is one to prove Jewish anteriority if one has to give up the patriarchal and Mosaic traditions?

This, then, was his dilemma. Demetrius was to find its solution in the works of Eratosthenes of Cyrene, chief librarian of the Alexandrian Library under Ptolemy III, and guardian of the king's son, the future Philopator. This friend of Archimedes, who knew the world was round and who had measured the length of the terrestrial circumference, with an error of a little more than one per cent (469 kilometers if we accept the value of 157,5 m. for the Greek stade), was the inventor of mathematical chronology.[72] His writings in this field brought order into Greek historiography. They may well have been at the root of the calendar reform undertaken by Ptolemy III which failed, and Julius Caesar's reform, which has had a lasting success. Demetrius was obviously his

---

[70]FGrH III 680, frg. 1,4.

[71]FgrH I, A, 1, 1a (frg. 13, p. 7-8).

[72]Recent reviews: J. Blomquist, "Alexandrian Science: The Case of Eratosthenes", in *Ethnicity in Hellenistic Egypt*, Aarhus 1992 (quoted above, note 36), p. 53-73 (with principal sources); C. Jacob, "Un athlète du savoir: Ératosthène", in C. Jacob & F. de Polignac, Eds., *Alexandrie, IIIe siècle av. J.-C.* (Autrement, Sér. Mémoires, 19), Paris 1992, p. 113-127.

disciple, either directly or because he had studied his works and adopted his methods.[73]

Demetrius follows the biblical text in the Greek version of the Septuagint, his sole source, and of which he is, moreover, the first historical witness. But one could search this text in vain for any sign of the profusion of dates and figures which fill his narrative. How could Moses have espoused Zipporah over a gap of three generations? How many years elapsed from the time of Adam to the entry of Joseph's kin into Egypt? From the flood to Jacob's arrival in Egypt? From Abraham to Jacob? The numerical answers to these questions aroused emotional responses in Demetrius' breast. Like Plato before him, in the *Epinomis* (976d– 979d), he is carried away by the science of numbers. On the other hand, the sacrifice of Isaac or Jacob's struggle with God leaves him cold; he relates these events in an appallingly jejune manner. The rape of Dinah and its subsequent revenge, that typically Mediterranean drama which can still make the hair on our necks stand on end when we read it today (Gn 34), is reduced, once again, in Demetrius' rendering, to a matter of figures: Dinah was sixteen years and four months old when Shechem raped her.

Demetrius' approach is much more radical than the priestly revision of the biblical *toledot*. He pretends to be strictly scientific, that is "philological," in the Alexandrian sense of the term coined by Eratosthenes. When the Greeks "discovered" the Jews, they saw them as a "people of philosophers" – the logical consequence of their monotheism which, for the Greeks, came under the heading of philosophical speculation and not of religious practice. This is what we read in the text of Theophrastus quoted above, the first element of a framework around which Greek thought was to erect its image of the Jew.[74] Later the Greeks took cognizance of other "extra-Hellenic philosophers": the Brahmans of India became for the Greeks the cousins or forebears of the Jews, who were to appear, in a genealogy, as offshoots of the main trunk of Oriental wisdom. Demetrius does not, however, consider himself a "philosopher," the repository of any sort of wisdom; he would like to be known as a "philologist," an artisan of knowledge, in the image of his guide, Eratosthenes, his best chance of obtaining credence. Who, indeed, could question the credibility of an historical

---

[73]I follow a suggestion of A. Swiderek, *The Gods came down from Olympus. Divinity and Myth in Greek Literature of the Hellenistic World* (Polish), Warsaw 1992, p. 287.

[74]See above, note 20. Cf. my art. "Image du Juif dans la pensée grecque vers 300 av. n.è.", in A. Kasher, U. Rappaport, G. Fuks, Eds., *Greece and Rome in Eretz-Israel. Collected Essays,* Jerusalem 1989, p. 3-14 (Hebrew), and 1990, p. 105-118 (French).

account cast in the sober, arid mold of a series of mathematical propositions, that supreme form of academic discourse?

Were he alive today, Demetrius would be able to set up his own computerized databank of biblical history. His efforts to use reputedly modern methods would certainly earn him academic support. Who knows if Brown University would not have offered him a chair in Judaic studies? Did he enjoy a similar success in Alexandria – for example, membership in the Alexandrian Museum and the personal congratulations of King Philopator, miraculously reconciled with the Jews after the failure of his murderous plot against them? History is silent on this point. But this sort of success story would have been more agreeable and less dangerous for an Alexandrian Jew than promotion to the priesthood was for Dositheus, his contemporary.

As to the presumed goal of his enterprise, Demetrius' exploit is illusory. In the long term, he may appear as a precursor, his history of the *Kings of Judea* heralding Josephus's *Jewish Antiquities*. The author of the *Book of Jubilees*, the author of the *Seder Olam Rabba*, Julius Africanus, Eusebius of Caesarea and others could be considered as his continuators.[75] In Alexandrian circles his efforts bore little fruit. The Jews of Alexandria surely preferred reading their Bible in the Greek text of the Septuagint rather than in the mathematical version of our chronographer. In Palestine, Eupolemus may have been an exception in this respect.[76] As for the Greeks, the scientific interpretation of the Torah held no more interest for them than the Torah itself. Much ado about nothing.

Dositheus' apostasy and Demetrius' torments are proof enough of the fact that, at a certain level in the social scale, dual allegiance could indeed be a problem. It was not always easy to be both a Jew and a Greek in Hellenistic Alexandria. But on the whole, this first experiment in diasporic adaptation developed in a fairly harmonious fashion. As full partners in a "colonial" enterprise, the Jews of Egypt were able to live out their Jewishness peacefully in terms of the Greek tongue and culture. This adventure was full of promise for the future. The West, through the action of Christianity, was to reap its harvest.

For the Jews, it ended in disaster. The Roman conquest of Egypt in 30 BCE transformed the previous situation from top to bottom. It sounded the death knell of the community of Hellenes. This sprawling group of individuals, neither "city" nor "nation," calling themselves

---

[75]E. Bickerman, "The Jewish Historian Demetrios", *Studies...* (above, note 68), p. 353.
[76]Sic B.Z. Wacholder, *Eupolemus. A Study of Judaeo-Greek Literature,* Cincinnati and New York 1974.

Greek and claiming citizenship, had no place in the new scheme of things. The Romans completely reorganized the body social, sorting out the Greek element by other (fiscal) means: the descendants of the Hellenes were promoted to the rank of privileged *ordines*.[77] For reasons which still remain mysterious, the Jews were set apart. Thus the Roman conquest of Egypt inaugurated a period of Jewish decline, which ended tragically in the destruction of Egyptian Jewry during the revolt of 115-117 CE.[78]

*

Two conclusions may be drawn from our reflections on this unique experiment of Alexandrian Jewry. Firstly, concerning the notion of diaspora, we may speak of a "Jewish diaspora" in Hellenistic Egypt while hesitating to apply the term "diaspora" to the Greco-Macedonian occupation of this country. Conquest and dispersion are two different things.

In the second place, one may, with hindsight, take the full measure of the decline of the Jewish diaspora in Egypt after the Roman conquest in 30 BCE. By tolerating the continuation of a double cultural allegiance, but prohibiting the Jews from being Greeks in the social and political sense of the word, the Roman Empire brought to an end the promising experiment initiated by the Ptolemaic monarchy. For future diasporas, the ups and downs of the Egyptian Jews during the Greek and Roman periods present considerable interest. They show that, given favorable circumstances, dual allegiance falls within the realm of possibility, but they give us due warning that, in the long term, it can prove dangerous. They also remind us that the success of any acculturation is closely

---

[77]See my study "Entre la cité et le fisc. Le statut grec dans l'Égypte romaine", in *Symposion 1982*, Valence 1985 (and Cologne 1989), p. 241-280 (= *Droit impérial et traditions locales dans l'Égypte romaine*, Aldershot 1990, no. I).

[78]V. Tcherikover, "The Decline of the Jewish Diaspora in Egypt in the Roman Period", Journ. Jew. Stud. 14, 1963, p. 1-32. See my *Juifs d'Égypte*, p. 131ff. (the Jews in Egypt under Roman rule) and p. 161ff. (the revolt of 115-117). Papyrological material on the revolt is collected by A. Fuks, CPJud. II, 1960, Section XI (Nos 435-450). More recently, the investigations of M. Pucci Ben Ze'ev deserve attention; see her book, *La rivolta ebraica al tempo di Traiano*, Pisa 1981, and her articles, "La rivolta ebraica in Egitto (115-117 d.C.) nella storiografia antica", Aegyptus 62, 1982, p.195-217; "CPJ II, pap. n. 158, pap. n. 435 e la rivolta ebraica al tempo di Traiano", Atti XVII Congr. intern. di Papirologia, Naples 1984, p. 1119-1123; "Greek Attacks against Alexandrian Jews during Emperor Trajan's Reign", Journ. for the Study of Judaism 20, 1989, p. 31-48. For new texts concerning the consequences of the revolt, see my art. Ἰουδαῖοι ἀφῃρομένοι La fin de la communauté juive en Égypte (115-117 de n.è.)", in Symposion 1985, Cologne 1989, p. 337-361.

linked to social and political status. It could be of vital importance for those who occupy positions of responsibility in our modern democracies to meditate upon the lesson that Alexandrian Jewry teaches us.

Abreviations

(other than Greek and Latin authors, as well as Biblical and Talmudic sources).

BGU VI = Ägyptische Urkunden aus den Königlichen (later : Staatlichen) Museen zu Berlin, Griechische Urkunden, Bd. VI: Papyri und Ostraka der Ptolemäerzeit, ed. W. Schubart and E. Kühn, Berlin 1922.

C.Ord.Ptol. = Corpus des Ordonnances des Ptolémées, ed. M.-Th. Lenger, Brussels 1964; 2nd edition, 1980, with a Supplement; 2nd Supplement, 1990.

CPR XIII = Corpus Papyrorum Raineri, Bd. XIII; Griechische Texte IX: Neue Papyri zum Steuerwesen im 3. Jh. v. Chr., ed. H. Harrauer, Vienna 1987.

CPR XVIII = Corpus Papyrorum Raineri, Bd. XVIII; Griechische Texte, XIII: Das Vertragsregister von Theogenis (P. Vindob. G 40618), ed. B. Kramer, Vienna 1991.

CPJud. : V. Tcherikover & A. Fuks, with the collaboration of M. Stern and D.M. Lewis in the third volume, Corpus Papyrorum Judaicarum, 3 vol., Jerusalem & Cambridge, Mass., 1957-1964.

CPJud. III App. I = Corpus Papyrorum Judaicarum, Vol. III, Appendix I: The Jewish Inscriptions from Egypt, by D.M. Lewis (reproducing, with necessary changes and additions, the Corpus Inscriptionum Judaicarum, ed. J.B. Frey, Vol. II, Vatican 1952, Nos. 1424-1539).

FGrH = F. Jacoby, Die Fragmente der griechischen Historiker, Berlin-Leiden 1923-1958.

Juifs d'Égypte = J. Mélèze Modrzejewski, Les Juifs d'Égypte, de Ramsès II à Hadrien, Paris 1991 and 1992.

P. Monac. III = Die Papyri der Bayerischen Staatsbibliothek München, Griechische Papyri, Bd. 3: Griechische Urkundenpapyri der Bayerischen Staatsbibliothek München, Teil 1 (Nr. 45-154), ed. U. Hagedorn, D. Hagedorn, R. Hübner, and J.C. Shelton, Stuttgart 1986.

P. Oxy. XLI = The Oxyrhynchus Papyri, Vol. XLI, ed. G.M. Browne, R.A. Coles, J.R. Rea, J.C. Shelton, E.G. Turner, and others, London 1972.

P. Ryl. IV = Catalogue of the Greek Papyri in the John Rylands Library, Manchester, Vol. IV: Documents of Ptolemaic, Roman and Byzantine Periods, ed. C.H. Roberts & E.G. Turner, Manchester 1952.

PSI XVII Congr. = Trenta testi greci da papiri letterari e documentari editi in occasione del XVII Congresso internazionale di Papirologia, Florence 1983.

P. Tebt. III/1 = The Tebtunis Papyri, Vol. III, Part 1, ed. A.S. Hunt & J.G. Smyly, assisted by B.P. Grenfell, E. Lobel & M. Rostovtzeff, London 1933.

Reinach, Textes = Th. Reinach, Textes d'auteurs grecs et romains relatifs au judaïsme, Paris 1895; reprint Hildesheim 1963.

Stern, Authors= M. Stern, Greek and Latin Authors on Jews and Judaism, 3 vol., Jerusalem 1976-1984.

V. Tcherikover, Prolegomena = V. Tcherikover, "Prolegomena," Corpus Papyrorum Judaicarum, I, Jerusalem & Cambridge, Mass. 1957, p. 1-111.

4

The Birth of a Diaspora: The Emergence of a Jewish Self-Definition in Ptolemaic Egypt in the Light of Onomastics[*]

Sylvie Honigman

The society of Ptolemaic Egypt was marked by a fundamental rift between the conquering minority, forming what is often called the "society of Hellenes," and the mass of the vanquished Egyptian peasantry, submitted to the traditional aristocratic and priestly classes.

[*]The present article uses material drawn for the most part from a paper which I wrote for the *Académie des Inscriptions et Belles-Lettres* (Paris) during a stay made at the French *Ecole Biblique* in Jerusalem, thanks to a Lagrange scholarship from the French Ministery of Foreign Affairs; in writing it, I profited by a number of corrections which Professor A. Caquot (*Collège de France*, Paris) was kind enough to suggest to me concerning the previous work.

I wish to thank more particularly my advisor, Professor J. Mélèze-Modrzejewski (University of Paris-I), who encouraged me to write this article and whose remarks contributed greatly to improve it. My thanks go also to Professor Leah Di Segni, of the Hebrew University of Jerusalem, who agreed to read an earlier draft, as well as to Professors D.R. Schwartz and I.F. Fikhman, of the Hebrew University, who gave me access to several publications during my last stay in Jerusalem and made valuable remarks of which I have made use here. Last but not least, warm thanks go to my friends Marc Naimark and Patricia Simonson who most kindly corrected my English text. Additional revisions of the English text were introduced by the co-editor of this volume, Professor Shaye J.D. Cohen.

Complete references to abbreviated titles are listed at the end of the article.

The term "Hellenes," which appears in the sources, reflects an ethnically mixed composition of the privileged society: it included all those who were able to claim a foreign origin and were, in Egypt, at the service of the Macedonian king, that is, not only the Greeks proper, but also all the people previously held as mere Barbarians: Thracians, Illyrians, Syrians, or Jews, all collectively opposed to the native population.

The gap between both societies, the conquering and the conquered, was of course partly socio-economical, but it was above all socio-juridical. The dichotomy was reflected first of all in the twofold judicial system set up by Ptolemy II Philadelphus in 275-272 BCE: courts of Egyptian priests, the "laocrits," were established to judge the native population according to the "law of the country" (*nomos tēs chōras*), while the population deemed Hellenic – among which, the Jews – depended on a "juridical *koine*" inspired from the Greek tradition and applied by the courts of "dicasteries" and by royal judges, the "chrematists," either as a written law in the framework of the three *poleis* which Egypt numbered, or as a customary law in the countryside.[1]

The opposition of socio-juridical status was underlined by the use of a different nomenclature in official documents: a "Hellene" was bound to state his name, patronym and ethnicon, that is, his geographic origin from outside Egypt. For this last item, an Egyptian substituted his place of residence. Thus, while the native defined himself by referring to his village community, the "foreigner" stressed the personal ties which bound him with the conquering king – not with the land.[2]

Considered from this general point of view, the differences that may have opposed the Jews to the "Greeks" stood on an only secondary level.

---

[1]See H.J. Wolff, *Das Justizwesen der Ptolemäer (Münchener Beiträge zur Papyrologie*, 44, Munich, C.H. Beck'sche Verlagsbuchhandlung, 1970[2]), with the precisions brought by J. Modrzejewski, "Zum Justizwesen der Ptolemäer," *Zeitschr. d. Savigny-Stift. f. Rechtsgeschichte, Rom. Abt.* 80 (1963), p. 42-82 and "Nochmals zum Justizwesen der Ptolemäer," *ibid.*, 105 (1988), p. 165-179. On laocrits and chrematists, see J. Modrzejewski, "Chrématistes et laocrites", in *Le monde grec. Hommages à Claire Préaux* (Paris, de Boccard, 1975), p. 699-708 and H.J. Wolff, *Das Problem der Konkurrenz von Rechtsordnungen in der Antike* (Heidelberg, 1979), p. 61-64.

[2]The pioneering article on this issue is E.J. Bickerman, "Der Heimatsvermerk und die staatsrechtliche Stellung der Hellenen im ptolemäischen Ägypten," *Archiv für Papyrusforschung* 8 (1927), p. 216-239. This study has since been completed and updated by J. Mélèze-Modrzejewski, "Le statut des Hellènes dans l'Egypte lagide: bilan et perspectives de recherches," *Revue des études grecques* 96 (1983), p. 241-274 (who adopted a somewhat different perspective from Bickerman's in his conclusions). Again, E.J. Bickerman, *The Jews in the Greek Age* (Cambridge, Mass./London, Harvard UP, 1988), p. 83-85.

Whatever their degree of religious particularism, the Jews were first and foremost a fully-fledged component of the class of "Hellenes."

Concretely, it is impossible to point to any specific connotation that would have distinguished the ethnic designation *Ioudaios* in the Egyptian context of the third century BCE. Certain individuals called themselves *Ioudaioi*, as others *Thraikes*, Thracians, or *Krētoi*, Cretans. Modern attempts to oppose the Jews to the other Hellenes by supposing that the former possessed their own autonomous organization are merely speculative. Neither was the class of Hellenes internally divided into separated groups which, according to modern claims, would have been as numerous as its ethnic components.[3]

This clear picture blurred somewhat by the second century, with the appearance of "pseudo-ethnica." These were above all connected to military circles.[4] From Ptolemy IV Philopator's military reforms on, ca. 222 BCE, the ethnic label, as far as it was connected with the army, was no longer a personal element, but was rather attached to a specific military unit, usually distinguished by its equipment.[5] But this

---

[3]See now J. Mélèze-Modrzejewski, *Les Juifs d'Egypte de Ramsès II à Hadrien* (Paris, A. Colin, 1992), p. 69-71; the old view was followed, among others, by V. Tcherikover, *The Jews in Egypt*, p. 95-98 (with the corresponding English summary of the fourth chapter), where the scholar gives a four-part presentation of the Graeco-Egyptian society; it was recently developed to an extreme by A. Kasher, *The Jews in Hellenistic and Roman Egypt. The Struggle for Equal Rights* (*Texte und Studien zum antiken Judentum*, 7, Tübingen, J. C.B. Mohr [Paul Siebeck], 1985). Kasher's theory on the autonomous organization of the Jews inside a *politeuma*-framework does not stand in the face of the documentation. See J. Modrzejewski, "La règle de droit dans l'Egypte ptolémaïque," in *Essays in Honor of C.B. Welles* (*American Studies in Papyrology*, 1, New Haven, 1966), p. 125-166, esp. 141-149 and C. Zuckerman, "Hellenistic Politeumata and the Jews. A Reconsideration," *Scripta Classica Israelica* 8-9 (1985-88), p. 171-185, who traces the history of this modern erroneous conception.

[4]See J. Lesquier, *Les Institutions militaires de l'Egypte sous les Lagides* (Paris, Leroux, 1911), pp. 88-90, 142-151, with C. Zuckerman's reservations, *loc. cit.*, p. 177, n. 14; M. Launey, *Recherches sur les armées hellénistiques*, I (Paris, de Boccard, 1987²), p. 63-64.

[5]Polybius, XXX, 25, describing a military march in the Seleucid empire, mentions Mysian, Thracian and Galatian units among others referred to by the technical name of their armament. This may have meant soldiers recruited in the military settlements of Syria, especially the Thracian ones, but may also refer to units armed "in the way of." See F.W. Walbank, *A Historical Commentary on Polybius*, III (Oxford Clarendon Press, 1979), p. 449-450. In Egypt, we can trace several soldiers who received a new ethnicon by changing of military unit. See Lesquier, *op. cit.*, p. 107. The first known example J. Lesquier can rely on is from 145 BCE, but the scholar dates the beginning of the phenomenon back to Ptolemy IV's new arrangements, "which deeply modified the general character of the monarchy and of the army."

evolution, which affected several ethnic designations such as "Macedonian," "Thracian," "Cretan," did not apply to *Ioudaios*. For, since it is impossible to demonstrate the existence of such a military specialisation, either in the equipment or in the costume, that could have justified the constitution of separate Jewish units, there are no grounds to think that the term *Ioudaios* underwent this kind of semantic shift. Thus, the ethnic value of the *Ioudaios* designation remained valid all through the Hellenistic age. The only problem connected to this term that could possibly arise is that of proselytism. Recent studies tend to prove that pagan sympathizers of the Jewish worship were named *Ioudaioi* in ancient sources.[6] R. Kramer has even raised some doubts about the actual ethnic identity of the two *Ioudaioi* who left a votive inscription in the temple of Pan at Redesiyeh (p. 46).[7] This is not, however, the most convincing part of her argument.

As the ethnicon played an important part in the definition of the individual's personal status in the Ptolemaic period, it is accordingly often found in the documents of this time; conversely, its use became exceptional under the Roman administration, when the mention of this datum was no longer required for administrative purposes.[8] The disappearance of the ethnicon of juridical value (as well as of the military pseudo-ethnica) was, of course, a direct consequence of the destruction of the class of Hellenes by Augustus. It may be illustrated by the example of the "Thracian" designation: while very common in the documents of

---

[6]See S. J.D. Cohen, "Crossing the Boundary and Becoming a Jew," *Harvard Theological Review* 82 (1989), p. 13-33, p. 21; R.S. Kramer, "On the Meaning of the Term "Jew" in Greco-Roman Inscriptions," *ibid.*, p. 35-53. We are faced with a similar problem in the cases of explicit mentions of persons liable to the Jewish tax, which was levied on Jews for the rather short time ranging from 70 CE to the almost complete annihilation of the Jewish community of Egypt in 115-117. The tax concerned not only the Jews by birth, but also, certainly, the proselytes and, according to Suetonius, at least under Domitian, the sympathizers of the "Judaic rites" (Suetonius, *Domitian*, 12). See L.A. Thompson, "Domitian and the Jewish Tax," *Historia* 31 (1982), p. 329-342.

[7]*CPJ*, III-App. I, 1537-1538 = A. Bernand, *Le Paneion d'El-Kanais. Les inscriptions grecques* (Leiden, E.J. Brill, 1972), nos. 34, p. 95-97 and 42, p. 105-109.

[8]In Roman times, a person was either citizen of one of the three – and later four – Greek *poleis*, or an "Egyptian," as such liable to the personal tax, the *laographia*; the privileged status conceded to the Greek inhabitants of nome capitals, according to which they paid the *laographia* at a lesser rate than the Egyptians proper, was no more than a secundary arrangement within the new socio-legal partition. See S.L. Wallace, *Taxation in Egypt from Augustus to Diocletian* (New York, 1938), pp. 109 ff., 116 ff.; J. Modrzejewski, "Entre la cité et le fisc: le statut grec dans l'Egypte romaine," in F.J. Fernández Nieto (ed.), *Symposion 1982. Vorträge zur griechischen und hellenistischen Rechtsgeschichte, Santander 1982* (Valencia, 1989), p. 241-280.

the Hellenistic period, especially in connection with military settlers, the Thracian ethnicon is no longer attested in the papyri of the subsequent Roman period, even though proper names of Thracian origin remain relatively common.[9]

In this context, an ethnicon in a papyrus of Roman times assumes a completely different meaning from one in the Ptolemaic period. Most often, its use indicates that the person thus qualified was either a foreigner or a recent immigrant whose foreign origin was still vividly felt in his new location. But it can also appear in connection with a person settled in Egypt for a long time: in such cases, it survived merely as a nickname stressing a strong ethnic peculiarity; for example, an "Ethiopian," to say a Black. Or, the term actually pointed to an occupation: thus, an "Arab" may be, according to the context, either a policeman or a shepherd; likewise, an Indian was an elephant keeper.[10] An interesting case is that of the Persian designation. Around the first century BCE, the phrase "Persian of the descent" (*Persēs tēs epigonēs*) became a legal fiction defining the situation of a debtor. It may even be found together with another ethnicon, when the debtor was a Hellene.[11]

---

[9]For the ethnic designation, see the list of occurrences, set in chronological order, in the *Dizionario, s.v.*, as well as the two lists of Thracians attested in Egypt, one for Ptolemaic, the other for Roman times, by V. Velkov and A. Fol, *Les Thraces en Egypte gréco-romaine* (*Studia Thracica*, 4, Sofia, 1977), pp. 22-72 and 72-96, which follow the alphabetic order of the names and mention the presence of the ehnicon whenever relevant. The contrast between both lists is striking: the only two instances of a mention of the ethnicon in the Roman sources (nos. 411 and 445) relate to soldiers. One of these, who left his name on a *syringe* in Thebes, explicitly stated his belonging to the *ala II Thracum equitata*; the man defines himself as "Thracian and Egyptian" (Θρᾷξ κεγύπτιος. See J. Lesquier, *Les Institutions militaires* [above, n. 4], p. 95-96).

[10]That an "Arab" was in fact a policeman follows from several Ptolemaic sources: see *P. Hamb.*, I, 105, verso, l. 2; *P. Cair. Zen.*, II, 59230, l. 4. Ann E. Hanson has recently demonstrated the meaning of "shepherd": see her article, "Egyptians, Greeks, Roman, *Arabes* and *Ioudaioi* in the First Century AD Tax Archive from Philadelphia. *P. Mich. Inv.* 880 Re. and *P. Princ.*, III, 152 Revised," in *Life in a Multi-cultural Society. Egypt from Cambyses to Constantine* (*The Oriental Institute of the University of Chicago Studies in Ancient Oriental Civilization*, 51, Chicago, 1992), p. 133-145. The twofold employment as shepherd and agent assumed by one Pnepheros in *P. Mich. Inv.* 880 Re. (Hanson, p. 138), probably appears again in a private letter of 41 CE (*BGU* 1079 = W. *Chr.* 60 = *Select Papyri*, 107), where the messenger bringing the letter is simply referred to as "the Arab" (l. 7). On Indian elephant keepers, see M. Launey (above, n. 6), I, p. 588; A. Bernand and O. Masson, "Graffites grecs d'Abou-Simbel," *Rev. Ét. Gr.* 70 (1957), p. 24, no. 14 and, for a literary evidence, *I Maccabees*, V, 37.

[11]See J.F. Oates, "The Status Designation *Persēs tēs epigonēs*," *Yale Classical Studies* 18 (1963), p. 5-129; E. Boswinkel and P.W. Pestman, *Les Archives privées de Dionysios, fils de Képhalas (Pap. Lugd.-Bat., 22*, Leiden, E.J. Brill, 1982), p. 56-63.

The term *Hellēn* itself pointed to a member of the class of notables settled in one of the nome capitals.[12]

As to the Jews, the religious connotation becomes all the more apparent: as a juridical designation, *Ioudaios* was bound to disappear together with all the other "national" ethnica. It could survive only because it had undergone a semantic shift of its own. This involved not a military, but a religious connotation. This explains why, while absent from Roman administrative documents, like all the other ethnica, it still appears in private documents; but it is found mainly in literary sources, like Philo or Josephus.[13]

Thanks to the changes which took place, then, between one administration of Egypt and the subsequent one, we are able to trace the ins and outs of the process: from a purely geographical and legal designation in the third century, the term *Ioudaios* eventually acquired a prominent religious connotation. It is clear, however, that the evidence from Roman times merely brings to light an existing situation that had been prevailing for some time before. In Egypt then, the Hellenistic age had seen the birth of a specific Jewish identity.

At first sight, the evolution we have just traced among Egyptian Jews would merely echo a process well known for Judaea: the shift from a purely national and ethnic self-definition to a religious identity, which resulted in the introduction of conversion, – first applied on a large scale by John Hyrcanus I, after his conquest of Idumaea in 128 BCE.[14] It is not sure, however, that Egyptian Jews were satisfied with playing the part of

---

[12]See J. Modrzejewski, "Entre la cité et le fisc" (above, n. 8).

[13]As the two ethnic designations *Arabs* (Άραψ) and *Ioudaios* appear together in the papyri published and commented by Ann E. Hanson, *loc. cit.*, this close connection led her astray in her conclusions. She supposes that the survival of the two was due to the ethnic peculiarity of the "Semites." But why should "Semites" be more strongly individualized, as far as ethnicity is concerned, than Thracians or Illyrians, for instance, is not clear. What, beyond the linguistic affinity, makes the different "Semitic" groups so kindred as to justify a common fate is also obscure. In fact, the term "Arab" does not imply in Greek a mere ethnic connotation: it pointed above all to a way of life, nomadism, as is shown by the recurrent clichés connected to the "Arabs" in the Greek sources (but also, for instance, in the Bible): the life under a tent, the cattle raising, the caravan traffic. On these commonplaces, see P. Briant, *Etat et pasteurs au Moyen-Orient ancien* (Paris/Cambridge, Cambridge UP, 1982), p. 113-152. Add further *II Macc.*, XII, 10-12. The two meanings attested in the Graeco-Egyptian documentary sources, "shepherd" and "policeman" (probably of the desert) directly derived from these clichés. The bare ethnic connotation does not suffice, thus, to explain the survival of the *Ioudaios* appellation.

[14]See S. J.D. Cohen, "Religion, Ethnicity, and "Hellenism" in the Emergence of Jewish Identity in Maccabean Palestine," in P. Bilde *et alii* (ed.), *Religion and Religious Practice in the Seleucid Kingdom* (Aarhus UP, 1990), p. 204-223.

a mere receptacle for a process that would have been elaborated elsewhere, in the Palestinian homeland. We cannot dismiss out of hand the possibility that the evolution among the Egyptian Jewry involved original aspects – if only to meet the local conditions. The awakening of self-awareness among the Jews of Egypt, which no doubt accompanied the increasing uniqueness of their position within Ptolemaic society, would correspondingly be the consequence of a twofold trend: while the Egyptian Jews unquestionably remained submitted to a certain degree to the influence from the "metropolis" (to use Philo's term), their local conditions called for original, appropriate answers. These local conditions were, thus, responsible for creating a margin of independent development. If this could be proved, it would mean that, eventually, this process resulted in the transformation, out of a group of *Judaean* emigrés, into the *Jewish* community of Egypt – that is, the shift from the situation of an uprooted *ethnic group* to a *diaspora*.

The issue is to determine the precise nature and extent of this process. In fact, if we were able to grasp it more accurately, this could reveal what made the transformation possible, and would throw some light on the very foundation (or, at least, on one of the foundations) of the diaspora situation.

We intend here to lay down some lines of research in this direction, in the limits imposed by the sources. The first step is to try and refine the chronology of the process; if its starting point could be precisely determined, it would be easier to pinpoint the one or several causes behind it (at least the immediate ones). Finally, the study of the terms of this cultural transformation might help distinguish between outside influence and local originality in the formation of a Jewish self-definition in Egypt.

The first question we are faced with is that of the sources which might be used for the study of a diffuse process of this kind. The moment we no longer restrict ourselves to the situation which prevailed at Alexandria but rather widen the scope of the study to the countryside, the *chora*, we cannot be satisfied with the literary output of the Judaeo-Alexandrian circles. The mention of the ethnic label, as just seen, does not allow sharp chronological analysis within the Hellenistic period. We should consequently appeal widely to anthroponymy, with all the reservations associated with this most delicate kind of source.

1– The originality of the Jews of Egypt within the surrounding society revealed through anthroponymy

Because of the very nature of the documentary sources discovered in Egypt – census records, fiscal rolls, and so on – the onomastical documentation is particularly abundant. This fact prompted the scholars to try and exploit the anthroponymy for the study of the Ptolemaic society. The preliminary step was to determine how personal names could be used as an indicator of the bearers' nationality.

The conclusions that are still authoritative today are those W. Peremans has defined in several articles.[15] Relying on the data of a wide-ranging prosopographical study including all the inhabitants either of Egypt or of the Ptolemaic possessions outside it and classifying them according to occupation[16] (an element which helps us determine their social condition and often even their nationality), Peremans was led to the following conclusions: in the third century BCE, names reflect in most cases the nationality of the bearer; in the second and first centuries, contrary to the prevailing opinion among the early scholars of papyrology, the onomastical criterion remains widely trustworthy. But on the other hand, these conclusions are valid only for the society as a whole and do not predetermine particular cases: ethnic and, as a consequence, onomastical minglings are attested as early as the third century, and are more numerous the lower the social status.

The social studies on Ptolemaic Egypt focus mainly on the prominent issue of the relationship between the Hellenic and the Egyptian entities and its evolution through the centuries. This issue relates of course to the debate on the very nature of the Hellenistic society – a cultural melting pot or a two-tier society – which has preoccupied the scholars since J.G. Droysen first raised it.[17] In this perspective, W. Peremans

---

[15]W. Peremans, "Ethnies et classes dans l'Egypte ptolémaïque" in *Recherches sur les structures sociales de l'Antiquité classique (Caen 1969)*, (Paris, CNRS, 1970), p. 213-233, and "Sur l'identification des Egyptiens et des étrangers dans l'Egypte des Lagides," *Ancient Society* 1 (1970), p. 25-38. A good account of the issue and of its historiographical dimension is provided in K. Goudriaan, *Ethnicity in Ptolemaic Egypt (Dutch Monographs on Ancient History and Archaeology, 7*, Amsterdam, Gieben, 1988), p. 1-7.

[16]The *Prosopographia Ptolemaica* (nine volumes so far, *Studia Hellenistica* series, Leiden, E.J. Brill, 1950-1981). W. Peremans summed up his analysis of each volume's data in a series of papers issued in *Ancient Society* 2-10, 1971-81.

[17]The theory conceived by J.G. Droysen in the 19th century saw the mingling between the Greek West and the Eastern cultures as the core of Hellenistic civilization. It has been refuted as a myth by the following generation of scholars: see Cl. Préaux, "Réflexions sur l'entité hellénistique," *Chronique d'Egypte* 40 (1965), p. 129-139, who traces Droysen's work and progress of thought. As is well known, the debate was opened anew when the approach shifted from the issue of the integration of natives into the Greek *polis*-type cities to more diffuse processes (as, for instance, the influence of Greek thought on Eastern native theologies or the adaptation of Greek models at the service of a bold opposition to Hellenism.) See, on the best-documented Jewish case, M. Hengel, *Judaism and Hellenism* [Philadelphia, Fortress Press, 1974]. On contemporary trends in Hellenistic

regrettably did not feel necessary to sort out by a more detailed analysis the general category of names he defines as "foreigner." In fact, generally speaking, monographs dealing with specific elements of the society of Hellenes are rare.[18] But some general principles may nonetheless be established in keeping with the method implemented by W. Peremans.

This scholar holds mixed marriages as the main cause of "abnormal filiation" – a phrase referring to an existing discrepancy between the ethnic origin of the names of an individual and his father. Mixed marriages remained relatively unusual between the two main socio-juridical entities of Egypt, except in the lower classes, but were characteristic of the relations among the Hellenes. For example, *P. Elephantine* 1, one of the most ancient Greek papyri of Egypt (310 BCE), is a contract of marriage between a man of Temnos and a woman of Cos. All restrictions to unions with foreign women which marked many of the classical Greek cities, like Athens, no longer applied in the heterogeneous societies of the Eastern Hellenistic kingdoms, which were lands of immigration.[19]

As a result of the new social reality of Ptolemaic Egypt, the mingling of the onomastical traditions between the various groups of immigrants was eventually unavoidable, proper names consequently losing the indicative value they may have retained more clearly in the more conservative (and nationalist) cities in Greece itself.[20] Since detailed

---

studies, see F.W. Walbank, "The Hellenistic World: New Trends and Directions," *Scripta Class. Isr.* 11 (1991/92), p. 90-113.

[18]The starting point most often remains the prosopographical lists of immigrants, presented in alphabetical order of the ethnica, gathered by F. Heichelheim, *Die auswärtige Bevölkerung im Ptolemäerreich* (Leipzig, 1925; additions in *Archiv für Papyrusforschung* 9 [1930], p. 47-55 and 11 [1939], p. 54-64, re-issued in 1963). For the later evidence, see the *Dizionario*. M. Launey, *Recherches sur les armées hellénistiques* (above, n. 4), covers only the military circles. W. Peremans' studies are not the last word about the opposition between Hellenes and Egyptians. They have on the contrary prompted many others, but all focus on this dichotomy. See K. Goudriaan, *op. cit.* (above, n. 15).

[19]See J. Mélèze-Modrzejewski, "Un aspect du "couple interdit" dans l'Antiquité. Les mariages mixtes dans l'Egypte hellénistique," in L. Poliakov (ed.), *Le Couple interdit. Entretiens sur le racisme, actes du colloque de Cerisy-La-Salle, 1977* (Paris/La Haye/New York, Mouton éditeur, 1980), p. 53-73, p. 57 f.

[20]L. Robert dedicated many papers to demonstrate that Greek proper names possessed a local coloration allowing, at least in series, to determine the geographical origin of a bearer or of a group of bearers; he correspondingly developed his thoughts on the implementation of personal names as a historical source. See, among others, "Epigraphie et antiquités grecques," *Ann. Coll. France* 62 (1961-62), p. 341-348; "De Delphes à l'Oxus. Inscriptions grecques nouvelles de la Bactriane," *Comptes Rendus de l'Acad. des Inscr. et Belles-Lettres* 1968, p. 416-457,

studies are lacking however, the analysis cannot go beyond general postulates. A distinction should probably be necessary between widely fashionable Greek names, such as dynastic or religious names, and others more peculiar and, as such, more likely to have retained an ethnic value longer.[21] The social networks which can be detected here and there among immigrants coming from the same city or the same area[22] certainly involved matrimonial ties; they may have lasted beyond the first generation, which would delay consequently the shift to the wide stock of personal names common to the whole Greek speaking population of Egypt. But in the long term, the differences were certainly bound to blur.[23]

Within this general framework, were there some ethnic groups which, like the Jews, preserved their identity? The few modern studies available provide two possible comparisons with Jews. When John Hyrcanus I conquered Marisa, a group of Idumaeans fled to Egypt, where they organized themselves as a *politeuma* in Memphis. These exiles were characterized by their will to assimilate into the surrounding Greek society; as D.J. Thompson-Crawford showed, this attitude eventually led, over three generations, to the drastic abandonment of national proper names.[24]

As the Thracian immigrants were essentially mercenaries, the study by M. Launey (I, p. 366-398) will suffice for the present purpose. Thrace represented a huge market for mercenaries from which first Alexander, and later the diadochs, repeatedly drew. Thracian colonies are attested

---

p. 433-435; "Samothrace 2.1: Fraser, The Inscriptions on Stone," *Gnomon* 35 (1963), p. 50-79.

[21]L. Robert, "De Delphes à l'Oxus...," p. 435, thus demonstrated that Kineas, son of Dositheos, a former officer and an eponymous priest of Ptolemy VI and Cleopatra I in Ptolemais in 173/172, was of Thessalian stock, as his name proves, and not Jewish, as suggested by J. IJsewijn because of the name of his father. See J. IJsewijn, *De sacerdotibus sacerdotiisque Alexandri Magni et Lagidarum eponymis* (*Verhandelingen van de Koninklijke Vlaamse Akademie voor Wetenschappen, Letteren en Schone Kunsten van België, Klasse der Letteren*, 42, Bruxelles, 1961), p. 44-47, nos. 110-117, and commentary, p. 100-101. See now W. Clarysse, G. Van Veken and J.P. Vleeming, *The Eponymous Priests of Ptolemaic Egypt* (*Pap. Lug.-Bat.*, 24, Leiden, E.J. Brill, 1983), p. 45.

[22]The Zenon archives provide a good example of such connections. See *P. Cair. Zen.*, I, 59021, quoted and commented by Cl. Orrieux, *Les papyrus de Zénon. L'horizon d'un Grec en Egypte au IIIe s. avant J.-C.* (Paris, Macula, 1963), p. 51: three fellow-citizens implored Zenon to present them with a letter of recommendation for the minister of finance at the court, Apollonios.

[23] A fact which is probably proved by the Thracian name of *Seuthes*. See further.

[24]Dorothy J. Thompson-Crawford, "The Idumaeans of Memphis and the Ptolemaic Politeumata," *Atti del XVII° Congr. Int. di Papirologia* (Naples, 1984), p. 1069-1075, p. 1072.

in the Fayûm as early as the reign of Ptolemy II Philadelphus. The recruitment of these mercenaries increased with the occupation by Ptolemy III Euergetes of several spots on the Thracian coast in the second half of the third century. Thus, the very high rate of native names borne by Thracian settlers in Egypt during the third century BCE was more a consequence of a continuous immigration than the sign of their retaining national traditions over several generations.[25] Under Ptolemy V Epiphanes, the loss of Thrace put an end to this continuous influx. Unfortunately, the evolution of the Thracian immigrants' offspring is hard to follow, since after ca. 220 the military ethnica, and the "hipparchy of Thracians" among them, became meaningless regarding the actual origin of the soldiers (Launey, p. 376). Launey observes, however, the increasing use of Greek names instead of indigenous ones, during the second century, in the still very active Thracian settlements (p. 386-387): "thus, only three indigenous names are found in the Hermopolis (Magna) stela [*SB*, I, 599], although there were no doubt more than three Thracians in this garrison in the second century."[26]

It seems then that the Thracians did not escape the general trend. It may even be suspected that the typical Thracian name *Seuthes* no longer pointed to Thracians by Roman times but had eventually slipped into the common stock of Greek proper names. Though the point escapes V. Velkov and A. Fol in their study on Thracians in Egypt, the name *Seuthes*, strikingly enough, represents no less than 43 of the 162 entries of the second prosopographical list, which covers the Roman period (a figure which represents in fact much more than one quarter, given the many dubious or even quite erroneous cases the list includes).[27] It is hard to

---

[25]For the data, see Launey, pp. 372 and 374-375. On the still mainly indigenous proper names borne by the inhabitants of the Pito settlement, south of Memphis, in 273, see U. Wilcken, *Archiv für Papyrusforschung* 3 (1906), p. 385, n. 321. However, the opposition Wilcken sees between this document from the first half of the third century and the Thracians mentioned in the *P. Petrie* file, from the second half of the century, is farfetched. Wilcken evidently tries to fit the sources to a preconceived pattern.

[26]On the Thracians in Egypt, see also now K. Goudriaan, "Ethnical Strategies in Graeco-Roman Egypt", in Per Bilde (ed.), *Ethnicity in Hellenistic Egypt (Studies in Hellenistic Civilization*, 3, Aarhus University Press, 1992), p. 74-99, at 77-79. A careful statistical discussion allows him to demonstrate the "early and thorough Hellenization of the Thracians as shown by their personal names." Note that Goudriaan too uses the example of the Thracians as a counterpart to the situation of the Jews.

[27]V. Velkov and A. Fol, *op. cit.* (above, n. 9). This work is badly weakened by ideological prejudices. See J. Bingen, "Les Thraces en Egypte ptolémaïque," *Pulpudeva. Semaines philippopolitaines de l'histoire et de la culture thraces*, 4 (1980,

believe that this name would have known a corresponding popularity in Thrace itself.[28] Moreover, a certain Seuthes, son of Dositheos, pays the Jewish tax at Arsinoe in 73 CE (*CPJ*, I, 421, ll. 173, 195): his case lets us think that, at the end of the first century if not earlier, this name could be adopted by individuals of *any* ethnic identity. Spreading of the name beyond Thracian circles is indeed a clue of the initial strength of this ethnic group. But though the Thracians revealed themselves capable of influencing the surrounding society, this was accompanied with their concurrent progressive dissolution therein. Their use of national anthroponymy did not hold up over time.

Against this general background, the behavior of the Jews appears in striking contrast with the trends pervading the other ethnic communities of their surrounding world. On the one hand, the Hellenization of the onomastical habits had begun very early, at least in the cleruchic circles, which are the best documented: the rate of Greek names is very high indeed even in third century sources. But on the other hand, the national names never ceased to be used. V. Tcherikover even showed that the national Jewish anthroponymy not only remained in use, but even enjoyed increasing popularity over time.[29]

Is it now possible to sharpen the chronological development of the process through a study of proper names, and, especially, to determine the starting point of this discrepancy between the Jews and the surrounding Hellenic society?

2–The chronology: a methodological question

M. Hengel does not hesitate to connect the evidence of the sources with a very precise pattern of political events.[30] In light of the documents gathered in *CPJ*, I, he estimates that the rate of "Semitic" names among the Jewish settlers of Egypt amounts to a rough average of 25 percent for the third century, though the real proportion must have been actually

---

issued Sofia, 1983), p. 72-79. Further mistakes were corrected by J. Modrzejewski, *Archiv f. Papyrusforschung* 32 (1986), p. 104.

[28]See D. Detschew, *Die thrakischen Sprachreste* (Wien, 1957); W. Tomaschek, *Die alten Thraker. Eine ethnologische Untersuchung, II. Die Sprachreste* (Wien 1893-1894); V. Beseliev, *Untersuchungen über die Personennamen bei den Thrakern* (Amsterdam, 1970). Further bibliography is available in F. Papázoglou, "Structures ethniques et sociales dans les Balkans," *Actes du VIIe congrès international d'épigraphie grecque et latine, Constantza, 1977* (Paris/Buracest, Les Belles Lettres, 1979), p. 153-169.

[29]V. Tcherikover, *Prolegomena*, p. 27 and *The Jews in Egypt*, p. 181.

[30]M. Hengel, *Jews, Greeks and Barbarians. Aspects of the Hellenization of Judaism in the pre-Christian Period* (Fortress Press, Philadelphia, 1980), p. 85-103 = *Griechen und Barbaren. Aspekte der Hellenisierung des Judentums in vorchristlicher Zeit* (*Stuttgarter Bibelstudien*, 76, Stuttgart, 1976), p. 116-144.

lower, since bearers of Greek names are not detectable in the sources unless the ethnicon *Ioudaios* is stated. By the second century, Hengel states, the rate became somewhat higher. The swift process of Hellenization among the Jewish cleruchs in the third century is to be explained, in his opinion, by their integration into mixed military units. Conversely, the revival of Hebrew names in the subsequent century should be related to the setting up of independent units of Jewish mercenaries under Ptolemy VI Philometor (around the time of Onias IV and his supporters' immigration to Egypt, ca. 165); the consequent strengthening of the Jewish status in Egypt as well as the concurrent Maccabean uprising in Judaea would have fostered the awakening of the Jews' national awareness from 167 onwards.

The historical events referred to are perfectly accurate, but the analysis is probably too rigid.

M. Hengel does not specify the way he divides the documents between the third and the second centuries; it is therefore impossible to check his results precisely. However, it follows from his commentary that he relies mainly on *CPJ*, I, section III, dealing with soldiers and military settlers in the third and second centuries BCE (documents nos. 18 to 32).[31]

Whatever the accuracy of M. Hengel's figures, still, what matters is not so much the ethnic composition of the military unit, as he puts it, but the dwelling place, the *village* where both soldiers and civilians of the same ethnic origin lived together. In the analysis of a cultural phenomenon such as anthroponymy, it is artificial, for instance, to isolate *CPJ*, I, 22 and *CPJ*, 28, which concern military settlers from the Fayûm village Samareia, from *CPJ*, 128 and *CPJ*, 133 mentioning civilians from the same village at a contemporary date.[32] Now, a comparison of *CPJ*, I, 22 (201 BCE) with *CPJ*, I, 28 (155 or 144) shows a high rate of Hebrew names in both, two generations apart, even though both are too early for the local military reorganization or even the political changes in Judaea to have had any impact. The same conclusions can be drawn for another Fayumic village, Trikomia, by comparing *CPR*, XIII, 4, from the second half of the third century BCE, with *CPJ*, I, 24, from 174 BCE. In the context of these two villages (if we limit the study to the four documents, included in *CPJ*, that could be used by M. Hengel for Samareia), it must be admitted that the retention of Hebrew proper names (or their revival)

---

[31]Does then the 25% figure given by Hengel for the third century echo the 25% calculated by the authors of the *CPJ* on the 90 names of the whole section, including both the third and second centuries documents (*CPJ*, I, p. 148) ? The discrepancy between both assessments of the same result is troubling.

[32]*CPJ* 22: 201, and 128: 218 BCE. *CPJ* 28: 155 or 144 BCE, and 133: 153 or 142 BCE.

was not due to a direct influence from Judaea or to the military reorganization of the local Jewish units.

Conversely, in documents, either from the third or from the second century BCE, concerning villages where an important Jewish presence is not attested in the extant documentation, the rate of Hebrew names falls much lower. But as each document concerns only a few individuals, by definition, any statistical calculation becomes here conjectural.

As a matter of fact, it seems that the central idea of M. Hengel's analysis, that of a contrast between the situations prevailing in the third and in the second centuries, echoes a conception of V. Tcherikover (*Prolegomena*, p. 28). But this analysis suffers from the objection that Tcherikover relies mainly, for the third century, on the Fayûm papyri, while the second century documents cast a special light on Upper Egypt, thanks to the ostraca discovered there. This implies a geographical gap between the two groups of documents.

In the lack of any really comprehensive vision of the situation, it seems then impossible to draw any definite conclusions from the sources themselves. Since the sample of study is rather limited, any new document is likely to put all the results in question.[33]

However, it should be noted that M. Hengel may have concluded too quickly that the first impulse toward the revival of a national awareness among Egyptian Jewry was due to an outside event. Certainly the Maccabean uprising stimulated the process, and perhaps prompted it. On a political level, the relations between Egyptian Jewry and Judaea are indeed well documented.[34] But perhaps events of more local scope should also be taken into account to explain the Jews' growing peculiarity within the Ptolemaic society. The end of the third century was marked by a large-scale social and political crisis in Egypt, an immediate consequence of the recruitment of native Egyptian soldiers in the Ptolemaic army during the battle of Raphia in 217. The anthroponymy is of course of no help for enlightening the historical core recorded in *III Maccabees*, which relates in a very legendary way how Ptolemy IV Philopator, the victor of Raphia, subsequently launched a persecution against the Jews, either of Alexandria or of the whole Egypt, a bitter moment which turned out happily by the "miracle of the

---

[33]The recently published *CPR*, XVIII, 7-11 modify in fact all previous data and general outlook on the Samareia village.

[34]See M. Stern, "The Relations between the Hasmonean Kingdom and Ptolemaic Egypt in View of the International Situation during the Second and First Centuries BCE," *Zion* 50 (1985), p. 81-106 (in Hebrew) and "Judaea and her Neighbors in the Days of Alexander Jannaeus," *The Jerusalem Cathedra* 1 (1981), p. 22-46; E.M. Smallwood, *The Jews under Roman Rule from Pompey to Diocletian. A Study in Political Relations* (*S.J.L.A.*, 20, Leiden, E.J. Brill, 1981), pp. 34, 37 and 224.

hippodrome." Here is not the place to settle the blatant contradictions between the account of *III Maccabees* and that of Flavius Josephus, who dates the events much later, under Ptolemy VIII (*Against Apion*, II, 49-55).[35] It should be simply kept in mind that the onomastic study of the Samareia and Trikomia villages does not indicate a clear break between the periods before and after the Maccabean uprising: the revival (inasmuch as it existed) may have preceded it.

If the precise chronology and immediate grounds of this revival remain uncertain, its features might be more instructive: the element that will serve as an indicator may be, once again, onomastics, no longer in its quantitative dimension (that is, the increasing share of traditional names in the anthroponymy of Egyptian Jews), but in its very nature.

3–Differences from the onomastical fashions in Judaea: a margin of cultural independence

The first question is whether the Maccabean outbreak had any influence on name-giving among Egyptian Jews, as it did in Judaea itself.

The general features of Jewish onomastics in Palestine between 300/200 BCE and 200 CE are now well known, thanks to a thorough statistical study undertaken by Mrs Tal Ilan, who gathered and sorted the names of close to 2,000 male individuals.[36] She clearly demonstrated that, among the nine names most popular in Palestine, are the six of the Maccabean heroes, *Mattathias, Ioannes, Simon, Ioudas, Eleazar, Ionathes* (*I Macc.* II, 1-5). The six together form no less than 30 percent of the male population of Palestine.[37]

---

[35]In a recent synthesis, J. Mélèze-Modrzejewski has defended the *III Maccabees* version. See *Les Juifs d'Egypte de Ramsès II à Hadrien* (Paris, A. Colin, 1992), p. 117-127.

[36]T. Ilan, "Names of the Jews in the Second Commonwealth. A Statistical Study," M.A. dissertation of the Hebrew University of Jerusalem. The author told me she does not consider this work ready for publication, and is working on a completed and updated version. It should be noted that the very conception of the collection of data does not make possible a clear distinction between Hellenistic and Roman material. This limitation is partly due to the exploitation of the rabbinical literature, which is not always bound to an exact dating. Even with these reservations, it provides a much more comprehensive base of work than the *CIJ*, previously the only collection available. T. Ilan has issued a series of articles presenting the conclusions which can be drawn from the data collected. Whenever possible, the figures given below are taken from the table included in T. Ilan, "The Names of the Hasmoneans in the Second Temple Period," *Eretz-Israel* 19 (1987), p. 238-241, p. 238; if not, from her unpublished corpus of data.

[37]T. Ilan, "The names of the Hasmoneans."

This exceptionally high rate leads T. Ilan to conclude, echoing a surmise first expressed by W.R. Farmer,[38] that the inspiration of the names in fashion in Judaea was drawn not from the Bible but from contemporary events, that is, from the immediate historical, and not from the religious, dimension of collective identity; they were the names of the national heroes, in keeping with the Hellenistic model (just as the names of the main characters of the Macedonian conquest of the East, *Alexander, Seleucus, Antiochus, Ptolemaios*, printed their stamp on the Greek name-giving). The reaction against Hellenism adopted many of its aspects, a paradox now familiar to historians.

In the present state of the documentation on the other hand, these six names were far from being the most popular in Egypt. *Mattathias* is simply not represented, *Eleazar* is somewhat well attested only from the very end of the Ptolemaic period on, the only previous evidence being *CIJ* 1531.

This discrepancy between the Palestinian and Egyptian situations teaches us two things. It may first corroborate the accuracy of T. Ilan's thesis.   The theory's weakness is, as she herself admits, that the onomastical documentation becomes somewhat abundant in Palestine only after the Maccabean revolt. Being so lopsided, it prevents any real comparison with the period preceding the uprising, and the correlation between the impact of the historical event and the allegedly new predilection for the related names cannot accordingly be established in a totally verifiable way. The gap can be partly filled with the evidence from Egypt. First of all, as compared with Judaea, Egypt yields rather abundant documentation for the period ranging from the middle of the third to the middle of the second century BCE. Moreover, it is generally accepted that Jewish settlers of the Fayûm were in their wide majority the offspring of Judaean immigrants who had left their country of origin at the beginning of the Hellenistic period, either by the time of Macedonian conquest or soon after, in any case at a stage previous to the turning point of the uprising. Consequently, the Hebrew anthroponymy used by Egyptian Jews stemmed from the same stock as that of Palestine known from the second century onwards. It follows that the popularity of names like Matthatias and Eleazar, and more tentatively of the four

---

[38]W.R. Farmer, *Maccabees, Zealots and Josephus* (New York, 1956), p. viii. See also R. Hachlili, "Names and Nicknames of the Jews in the Second Temple Period," *Eretz-Israel* 17 (1984), p. 195-208, p. 191-192 (both quoted by T. Ilan, "The Names of the Hasmoneans").

other Maccabaean names also, seemingly started increasing in Judaea at a stage later than the formation of the Judaeo-Egyptian settlements, that is, probably after the revolt; for otherwise, these names should be found in Egypt in an equivalent proportion.

In another respect, the lack of symmetry between both Palestinian and Egyptian stocks definitely attests to a certain degree of independence of the Egyptian Jews towards Judaea: they did not just submit passively to influences coming from the homeland. In that respect, it clearly appears that the continuous exchanges between both neighboring areas were not solely responsible for the adherence of the Egyptian Jews to their national proper names (as it seems to have been the case for the Thracian mercenary circles).

If the movement of national reaction in the "metropolis" no doubt fostered the awakening of a national awareness among Egyptian Jewry and worked as a trigger, the precise form it assumed in each country was thus different; the Jews of Egypt were able to draw upon their own history, thus shaping their own collective identity. It may be possible to trace this process through the study of the proper names assumed by Jews – at least those names we would qualify as traditional, leaving aside the Greek names.

4–Delimiting the onomastical documentation

The true features of the national Jewish anthroponymy in Egypt cannot be defined without an accurate selection of the material. The identification of an individual as a Jew through the mere criterion of his name raises a twofold problem: it is first necessary to distinguish, among the persons who bore a Semitic name, those who were Jews from those belonging to another ethnic group. It must also be ascertained that the names held to be Semitic have been correctly construed; this last problem holds true especially for the names said to be Biblical.

The implications bear first on the strictly prosopographical level, since the establishment of the collection of data is based on this preliminary verification. But they also involve a cultural aspect, the issue at hand being the respective part of the scriptural influence and of the oral tradition in the choice of Hebrew names.

4.1–Extra-biblical Semitic names:
the identification of the nationality of the bearers[39]

Several categories of names must be distinguished, after V. Tcherikover (*The Jews in Egypt*, p. 180-181), among those used by Jews: Greek, common Semitic and Hebrew. As far as Greek and common Semitic names are concerned, the question is the correct identification of the bearer as Jewish. The context must be taken into account.

The case of Greek names should not detain us here, since it is familiar: it is now widely admitted that names such as *Dositheos*, *Theodoros*, and the like were not in use exclusively among Jews. Less attention has been paid, on the contrary, to the fact that the same kind of ambiguity arises with Semitic names.

The accurate assessment of the ethnic origin of a Semitic name requires us to pay attention to its relative spread in the various Semitic speaking areas, that is, to use a statistical approach. Whenever the name under consideration stems from a root that is not specific to Hebrew but is common to other Semitic languages, if no theophoric element is present that could reveal the precise nationality of the bearer, the name should be taken for Jewish only if it appears to be widespread in the Judaean sources (that is, epichoric to Judaea), while concomitantly seldom in the Eastern areas where the other Semitic languages concerned were spoken.[40] A new examination of the areas of distribution of some of these names may thus lead to the conclusion that the inclusion of several documents in the *CPJ* is erroneous. The name Gaddaios will serve as an example.

4.1.1–"Semitic name" and "Jewish bearer": *Gaddaios*

CPJ, I, 37 preserves a complaint written in 222 BCE by three farmers, Theodotos, Gaddaios and Phanias. Although he concedes that the name *Gaddaios* is common Semitic, V. Tcherikover endeavors to find evidence of it in Jewish onomastics. He first appeals to the Biblical occurrences of the name; but, against this, it can easily be observed that those do not belong to the same period and cultural background as the document

---

[39]In the quotations of names in Greek, the accent will be systematically noted only for names of Greek stock. For others, it will be noted only for literary instances or in the measure they fit a Greek declension. We shall refrain from noting it in other cases, in order to avoid inconsistency. The collections of sources used below for the onomastical analysis will be quoted in a very abbreviated form. Complete references are listed at the end of the article.

[40]For a methodological example, see the handling of the name Ḥanan by E.J. Bickerman, "The Generation of Ezra and Nehemiah," p. 10-14.

under consideration.[41] The Jewish epigraphical evidence of Graeco-Roman times is unsubstantial.[42] The rather meager result of this survey sharply contrasts with the comparatively abundant occurrence of the names derived from *Gad* in the Arabo-Syrian world.[43]

This is not surprising. Gad, or Jad, is the genius of Fortune, revered both by Syrians and Arabs.[44] *Gaddaios* no doubt renders *Gdy* or *Gdy,*' that is an anthroponym based on the name of this god, with a suffix of possession. By its meaning, it corresponds to *Eutychus* and *Fortunus*.[45] The popularity of this protecting divinity explains the ancient predilection for names that recalled him. Concurrently, for the Jews, in a time when the names of the Patriarchs were out of use, with some rare exceptions,[46] *Gaddaios* was not likely to evoke the eponymous name of the tribe of *Gad*, but could refer only to the pagan god. Their rejection of the name is thus easily understandable.[47] It is then most certain that

---

[41]J.D. Fowler, *Theophoric Personal Names in Ancient Hebrew. A Comparative Study* (*Journal for the Study of the Old Testament. Supplement Series*, 49, Sheffield Academic Press, 1988), p. 280, *s.v. Gd*, insists that, even in the Bible, the name was not specifically Jewish.

[42]Only two Jewish inscriptions can be quoted, one from the Gaza area, the other one perhaps from Caesarea, Γαδος and Γαδη (the latter treated as undeclinable, in an inscription dated on paleographical criteria between the middle second century CE and the middle third century. See M. Schwabe, *Bull. of the Jewish. Pal. Expl. Soc.* 10 [1942-43], pp. 79-81 and 105-108 [in Hebrew]). Schwabe is only able to indicate three further rabbinical examples (one *Gada'*, one *Gadya'* and one *Gadday*). To these may be added the nickname of one of Judah Maccabee's brothers, Ἰωάννης ὁ καλούμενος Γάδδης (*AJ*, XII, 266; the name is spelled Γαδδις in *AJ*, XIII, 10). Out of Palestine, an inscription from Porto, *CIJ*, I, 535, reveals a Γαδια, a leader of a Jewish community in Rome.

[43]J. Teixidor, *Inventaire des inscriptions de Palmyre*, fasc. XI, Beyrouth, 1965, p. 15, with bibliography; Stark, p. 13; Cantineau, p. 76; *Dura*, V, 1, Index. See also Γαδιας, an Idumaean noble, friend of Herod the Great, also called Ἀντίπατρος (*AJ*, XV, 252).

[44]See D. Sourdel, *Les Cultes du Hauran* (*Bibl. Hist. et Arch.*, 53, Paris, P. Geuthner, 1952), p. 49-52; J.G. Février, *La Religion des Palmyréniens* (Paris, Vrin, 1931), p. 36-46; R. Dussaud, *La Pénétration des Arabes en Syrie avant l'Islam* (*Bibl. Hist. et Arch.*, 59, Paris, P. Geuthner, 1955), p. 110; *P.W., s.v.* Gad (Fr. Cumont). Gad is also the protecting genius of the family.

[45]See Fowler, *op. cit.*, p. 280, *s.v. Gd*; Harding, p. 154, *s.vv. Jd* and *Jdd*; Cantineau, p. 76, *Gdw; Dura*, V, 1, *Gadus*; Benz, p. 294, with further evidence. Add Γαδδων in Tyre (quoted by J. Teixidor, "Bulletin d'épigraphie sémitique," *Syria* 55 [1979], p. 361, no. 42). Stark, *Gdy'* and *Gd'*, pp. 13 and 81, holds the latter for the godly name used as proper name, while the former is a hypocoristicon ("X… is my fortune," compare *Gdynbw*, "Nabû is my fortune").

[46]See further (§ 5).

[47]This is indirectly confirmed by a Tannaitic text from the Cairo Geniza published by S. Schechter in 1904 and quoted by D. Flusser, "Paganism in Palestine," in M.

Gaddaios in *CPJ*, I, 37 not only bore a Syrian name, but actually *was* a Syrian himself.

We can also consider the name *Theodotos* as the counterpart of a religious Syrian name. As abundantly proved by inscriptions, the names recalling higher divinities, Baal or Allah, often found an equivalent not only in Greek compounds of *Zeus* (whence the numerous *Diodotos* and *Zenodoros* in the East[48]) but also in the names including the *theo-* element.

The correspondence is even more relevant with abbreviated religious names, common in Arabic as well as in Aramaic, in which the divine name is understood: *Abdos/Abdaios, Zabdos/Zabdaios, Ausos, Alafos, Aouidos, Abibas, Zabinas* and the like. Greek names as *Theodoros* or *Theodotos* rendered in a very appropriate way the anonymous evocation of the god and were therefore very common in the Hellenized anthroponymy of Semitic speaking areas as early as the Hellenistic times.[49] In *CPJ*, I, 37, *Theodotos* could of course simply point to a Greek.

The scope of immigration of non-Jewish Aramaic (and Arabic) speakers to Egypt in the Hellenistic period (especially in the third century BCE) was wide enough to prevent the conclusion that the presence of a neutral religious name alongside common Semitic names in a papyrus indicates that all the members of a given group were Jewish. Accordingly, it can be doubted whether the three farmers Theodotos, Gaddaios and Phanias of *CPJ*, I, 37 have their place in the *CPJ* collection.[50]

Stern and S. Safrai (eds.), *The Jewish People in the First Century* (*Compendia Rerum Iudaicarum ad Novum Testamentum*, I/2, Assen-Maastricht, Van Gorcum/Philadelphia, Fortress Press, 1987), p. 1065-1100, p. 1075 and nn. 1 and 2: "of the pagan divinities it is said: "You shall destroy their names" (*Deut.*, 12:3). Change their names ! When you hear the name *Gadya*, call it *Gallya* (dung)" (translation by D. Flusser). *Gadya* is here placed by the Sages on the same level as *Pane-Baal* and a theophoric name of Kos.

[48]On the popularity of *Zenodoros* in Syria, see G.J. Toomer, *Greek, Roman and Byzantine Studies* 13 (1972), p. 180-185, p. 184, n. 32.

[49]See the comment by M. Sartre, *Bostra* (*Bibl. Hist. et Arch.*, 118, Paris, P. Geuthner, 1985), p. 206, *s.v.* Θεοδώρα/Θεόδωρς, who mentions as possible equivalents *Ausallas, Zabdallas, Ouaballas*, and so on. *Dura*, V, 1, p. 58 recalls that names such as *Theodoros, Theodotos, Theogenes, Theophanes, Theomnestos*, were widespread in the Syrian area. *Theodoros* and *Theophilos* appear in Semitic characters in Palmyrenian inscriptions (see Stark, *s.vv. Tydwr'* and *Typyls*, p. 117). The "pagan monotheism" (in fact, it would be more accurately defined as a henotheism) which underlied these names has been studied by J. Teixidor, *The Pagan God. Popular Religion in the Greco-Roman Near-East* (Princeton UP, 1977), in the Syro-Phoenician, North-Arabic (Nabataean) areas, as well as at Palmyra. See especially the introductory chapter, p. 13-18.

[50]The third name, *Phanias*, is Greek.

The entire issue can be summed up in one question: did the Jews bear, as V. Tcherikover thinks (*The Jews in Egypt*, p. 187), common Semitic names which they borrowed from other Eastern ethnic groups that immigrated like them to Egypt ?

4.1.2–Jews and Syrians: two distinct worlds

This statement by V. Tcherikover recalls a prejudice he expresses elsewhere (*Prolegomena*, p. 5; *The Jews in Egypt*, p. 17-20) according to which the Jews dwelt in the "Syrian villages" of the Egyptian *chora*, in the neighborhood of settlers from varied areas from Greater Syria; this closeness would have led the Jews to borrow Syrian names.

Tcherikover rightly reminds us that Judaea was part of the geographical entity called Syria-Phoenicia by the Greeks, whose inhabitants indistinctly received the appellation of "Syrians."[51] However, the examples quoted by Tcherikover to prove that Jews could be called "Syrians" bear on language[52] – which is after all justified, since Aramaic was widely spoken in Judaea – not on people. A confusion concerning persons could involve only isolated individuals: the Jews organized in colonies were called *Ioudaioi*, not *Syroi*. Moreover, a mixed dwelling of Jews and Syrians seems plausible only in the case of prisoners of war settled by force in the same spot.[53] There were no grounds for Jews to willingly share a common village with Syrian immigrants rather than with others; the opposite was most likely true. The intercommunal relations are known to have been bad in Palestine itself;[54] synagogues or temples to Syrian deities built in Egypt were not precisely the best suited places for brotherly feelings to awaken.

It should be added that the presentation of *CPJ*, I, 36 in the *Corpus* is misleading: according to the editors' commentary, the document

---

[51]*Prolegomena*, p. 5, n. 13. For Judaea as part of Syria, see also Philo, *Against Flaccus*, 39.

[52]*The Jews in Egypt*, p. 18, n. 15: the sources referred to are *P. Petrie*, III, 7 (*CPJ*, I, 126, from 238/7 BCE, republished by W. Clarysse as *P. Petrie²*, 14, p. 163-168), l. 14-16 and *Aristeas*, 11. It is not certain that the Greeks systematically confused the language with the ethnicity: Diodorus of Sicily, XIX, 96, 1, recounts that the Nabataeans besieged in Petra had sent to Antigonus Monophtalmus a letter written in "Syrian characters" (συρίοις γράμμασι), that is, in Aramaic. But he had no doubt that the Nabataeans were Arabs (XIX, 94, 1).

[53]Among the "Asiatic" ('Ασιαγενεῖς) prisoners; see *P. Tebt.* 853, introduction, from 173 BCE and *P. Tebt.*, III, 1001, second cent. BCE.

[54]In his relation of the anti-Jewish disorders that occurred in the Greek cities of the Palestinian coast in the years preceding the revolt of 70 CE, Flavius Josephus speaks of the Jews' enemies as "Syrians." See for instance *BJ*, V, 550 and 551, 556 (in *BJ*, II, 266, the term refers to the inhabitants of Caesarea and is occasionaly replaced by "Greeks").

allegedly shows the presence in the same work-team of both Jews (Ieab, a "*Joab*," is said to be "no doubt a Jew") and Syrians (Natanbaal and Ragesobaal cannot be but Syrians, since Jews refrained from bearing sacred names of Baal by this time). In fact, none of the names of the workers associated in this team points to a Jew. *Ieab* does not stand for the Yahwistic *Joab*, but is an abbreviated Aramaic name,[55] most probably a Syrian sacred name. *Chazaros* should not be linked to the family of Hezir (the *benei Hezir*); if the first editors gave the right explanation for it, the name could be Iranian.[56]

Even if the two occurrences of Jews settled in a "Syrian village" of the Egyptian *chora* were to be admitted (whose personal ethnicon, official or unofficial, is unfortunately unknown), the mutual borrowing of proper names does not come into consideration, for several reasons. First, the exchange of sacred names – which represented the greater bulk of the Eastern anthroponymy, as elsewhere in Antiquity – was not likely to happen between a monotheistic group and its heathen neighbors. Secondly, if they were to give up their national proper names, the Jews must have been more tempted to adopt the standard Greek names that assimilated them to the socially prominent group than other barbarian ones.

Finally and even more importantly, it has been previously seen that the traditional name-giving by Jews in Egypt was not continuous, but involved a process of awakening anew. If, then, the first generations of Jewish immigrants had brought these Aramaic names with them from their country of birth, as suggested elsewhere by V. Tcherikover (*Prolegomena*, p. 27), these names were certainly the first to fall out of

---

[55]Ιεαβ is a rough transcription of the Aramaic verb *yhb*, "to give." The name must thus be an abbreviated theophoric name meaning "X... has given." See Βαλιαβος (*SB*, V, 8066, 34), *Belihabus*, Ναβουιααβος at Dura (*Dura*, V, 1, p. 61, § C1), Κοσιαβος (Peters–Thiersch, p. 145, no. 13 = *SEG*, XXIV, 1488). *Ieab* may be compared to *Yhyb'*, past participle of the same verb, attested at Palmyra, which has the same meaning as the more common *Zbyd'* (A. Caquot *in* H. Ingholt, H. Seyrig, J. Starcky, *Recueil des Tessères de Palmyre* [Paris, 1955], p. 173, *s.v.*).

[56]For the Iranian interpretation, see F. Justi, *Iranisches Namenbuch* (Marburg, N.G. Elwert'sche Verlagsbuchhandlung, 1895), *s.v. Ḥazar*, quoted by Mahaffy. The occurrence of *CPJ*, I, 36 (= *W. Chr.* 198) is not included, however, in Ph. Huyse's lexicon, *Iranische Namen in den griechischen Dokumenten Ägyptens* (*Iranisches Personennamenbuch*, Bd. V, fasc. 6a, Verlag d. Österreich. Akad. d. Wiss., Wien, 1990). The Hezir family is mentioned in *I Chron.*, 24:15 and is also known from an inscription ornamenting the front of one of the monumental tombs of the Cedron valley in Jerusalem, *CIJ*, II, 1394. True, the Iranian name *Hazar* is rare, as objected by the *CPJ* authors, but so is *Hezir*, which is moreover known as family and not as personal name.

use.[57] When the bestowing of traditional names resumed, it is hard to believe that Syrian proper names suddenly revealed themselves attractive for the Jews, especially in the circumstances we have described above: the renewal of traditional naming among the Jews did not owe anything to the local trends of Egyptian society, but was connected to a nationalist reaction. The supposed daily intercourse with Syrians, who must have undergone themselves as swift a process of Hellenization as the Thracians or, later, the Idumaeans, must not have played an important part, if any, in this process.

It seems then more cautious to consider that a Syrian name points to a Syrian bearer, especially when it concerns a sacred pagan name such as *Gaddaios*.

If the revival of the Jewish onomastics in Egypt does not involve common "Semitic" anthroponymy, we must consider, conversely, the rôle of Biblical names in this process.

4.2–The Hebrew names: Biblical inspiration versus family tradition

The problem raised by Greek names – the neutral sacred names like *Theodoros* and some privileged equivalents of Jewish names, like Simon – as well as common Semitic names, concerns the link between a properly identified name and the corresponding nationality of the bearer. The problem involved is somewhat different in the case of names considered specifically "Jewish." If the name is accurately construed, then the identity of the bearer does not leave any doubt.[58] In such conditions, the problem is the (linguistical) analysis of the name itself: has the name under consideration been *confused* with a Hebrew one?

One clear fact must be underlined first: the increase in the use of the Biblical proper names, as undeniable as it is, involved a much more limited range of names than often believed. As compared with the greater fantasy of the Byzantine age, the onomastical stock in common

---

[57]Even this solution is not convincing however, unless one assumes a drastic drop of such names after the Maccabean uprising, whence the sources become more abundant – an assumption that would be plausible indeed, since it would fit the feature of religious reaction that characterized the revolt. In all events, the use of Syrian names in Judaea after the 160's is not confirmed by T. Ilan's statistical study.

[58]The adoption of Biblical names among the Christian circles in Egypt began much later and does not concern us here. See R.S. Bagnall, "Religious Conversion and Onomastic Change in Early Byzantine Egypt", *Bull. of the Amer. Soc. of Papyrology* 19 (1982), p. 105-124; E. Wipszycka, "La valeur de l'onomastique pour l'histoire de la christianisation de l'Egypte. A propos d'une étude de R.S. Bagnall," *Zeitschr. f. Papyrologie u. Epigraphik* 62 (1986), p. 173-181, responded to by Bagnall, *ibid.* 69 (1987), p. 243-250.

use during the Graeco-Roman period was much narrower. A thorough examination of most of the rare names held to be Biblical by modern scholars will reveal that they actually stem from a completely different origin, as the following example will show.

4.2.1–Anachronism in a name analysis: Samson and Nehemiah

In *CPJ*, II, 416, the restitution [Σαμ]ψαις 'Ι[ωσ]η[που], l. 13, is allegedly justified by the presence of two more Jewish names in the document, Νε[..]ειων 'Ιωση[που], l. 12, and [Μύσ]θας Σαμβαθίων(ος), l. 10. Again, in *CPJ*, II, 433, Σ[α]μψαῖο(ς) – Πετ[ε]χ[..] Σ[α]μψαίο(υ) – recto, col. II, l. 39), is taken for Jew because of the appearance of a 'Ιωσηπος, l. 34. In both cases, the name is connected (yet with some reservations) to the Biblical prototype *Shimshon, Samson,* transcribed Σαμψων in the Septuagint.   But even if the equivalence were acceptable from a phonetical point of view, such a restitution is historically inconceivable.[59] In the case of *CPJ*, II, 416, the accurate reading is that proposed by the first editors of the papyrus, A.C. Johnson and H.B. van Hoesen (*P. Princ.*, I, 2, col. III, l. 10), [Πομ]ψαις. *Pomsaïs* is an Egyptian name, theophoric of the god Shai.[60] The bearer was a Jew only as far as the reading of the father's name is accurate, but the case seems here rather sure (though it is very fragmentary in the document, the Greek names beginning with a *iota* are few, and it can reasonably be assumed that [Pom]psaïs was brother of Ne[..]eiôn, son of Iose[pos] mentioned in the following line).

As for the reading of the name in *CPJ*, II, 433 (= *BGU*, VII, 1635), it is very dubious. It seems then more satisfying to replace the restituted *alpha* by an *epsilon* and to think of another Egyptian name recalling the same god, Πεμψαϊς or Σενψαϊς.[61] It may then legitimately be doubted that a *Petech[on/onsis ?]* or *Petech[noubis/nouphis ?]*, son of a *Pempsaïs* or *Senpsaïs*, was a Jew, on the mere criterion of his name.

---

[59] Anthroponyms derived from the name of the sun god *Shams* were common in Phoenicia, in the Aramaic-speaking area and in the Arab world. One can recall Sampsigeramos, King of Emesa, whose name means "the sun has decided (the birth of the child)," spelled Σαμψιγεραμος in the manuscripts tradition of Strabo's writings (XVI, 753), and Σαμψικεραμος in Flavius Josephus (*AJ*, XVIII, 5, 4 and XIX, 8, 1). For literary evidence, see W. Pape/G.E. Benseler, *Wörterbuch der griechischen Eigennamen* (Braunschweig, 1884[3]), *s.v.*; some epigraphical occurrences attest the first spelling, *SEG*, XXVI (1976), 1643 and XXXV (1985), 1504. Understandably enough, these theophoric names of the sun god do not come into consideration here, if the individual is to be considered a Jew.

[60] See Hopfner, p. 46, § 60; J. Quaegebeur, *Le dieu égyptien Shaï dans la religion et l'onomastique* (*Orientalia Lovaniensia Analecta*, 2, Louvain, 1975; *non vidi*).

[61] Hopfner, *ibid.*

The restoration Νε[εμ]ειων in *CPJ* 416 is less hazardous, since the name Nehemiah is well evidenced in the Persian period and was still borne in Judaea in Hellenistic times[62], even though it has not yet been attested in Egypt. But it relies on a phonetical approximation as compared with the reading of the Septuagint, where the name is spelled Νεεμίας. It is more cautious then to think of the spelling variant of a Greek name, Νε[μ]είων, *Νε[ιλ]είων, or *Νε[μεσ]είων, according to what is best suited for the lacuna width.[63]

4.2.2–The influence of the Bible: a chronological perspective

By the beginning of the Hellenistic age, Yahwistic names, "constructed as statements [indicating] the hopes and beliefs of the parents"[64] and reflecting the religious aspirations of the "generation of Ezra and Nehemiah," to quote E.J. Bickerman, began to decline in popularity. This decline corresponded to a profound shift in religious feeling.

Conversely, the emergence at this point of names inspired from the Bible can be easily explained. From the Hellenistic period onwards, or perhaps from a slightly earlier time, the Bible began to assume the character of a closed corpus, serving as a reference and starting point for a wide-ranging exegetical literature. The revival of onomastical habits pointed out by V. Tcherikover is thus correlative to the emergence of the Apocrypha and Pseudepigrapha, which characteristically stand in an external relationship to the Biblical texts themselves. Compared to the Biblical corpus, the apocryphal and pseudepigraphical writings represent a "post-classical period."[65] As the study of the Scriptures developed in the newly emerging synagogues, it should not seem surprising that this process of reference soon spread beyond purely learned circles and was manifested in daily life by a new taste for Biblical proper names.

---

[62]Six instances according to T. Ilan, *Eretz-Israel* 19, table 1, and "Names of the Jews": among others, one of R. Aqiva's disciples (last generation before Bar-Kosiba's uprising), *m.Terumot* 8:7; one ossuary, *CIJ*, II, 1220.

[63]See the *Namenbuch* and the *Onomasticon*, s.vv. Νεμείων (besides Νεμείας, Νεμέας), Νειλίων, Νεμεσίων and, for the latter, Fraser–Matthews, p. 325, s.v. The spellings *Νε[ιλ]είων and *Νε[μεσ]είων are not attested as such, but ει for ι was very common. See F.T. Gignac, *A Grammar of the Greek Papyri of the Roman and Byzantine Period, I. Phonology* (*Testi e documenti per lo studio dell'antichità*, 55b, Milano, Cisalpino-Goliardica, 1976), p. 189-191.

[64]E. Bickerman, "Ezra–Nehemiah," p. 16.

[65]This analysis of the apocryphal and pseudepigraphic literature as well as its suggestive definition as a "post-classical" literature is borrowed from M. Kister, lecturer at the Hebrew University of Jerusalem.

A break comparable to that which occurred between the Persian and the Hellenistic eras is perceptible from the second century CE onwards. Some further Biblical names then came into use, but the change was marked above all by a shift in the relative popularity of the names. That this shift was a general one, the sources bear witness: in Palestine, the inscriptions from the Jewish necropoles at Jaffa and Beth-Shearim as well as the Rabbinic literature;[66] in the diaspora, those of Asia Minor or Italy, two particularly well-documented areas.[67] Clearly, the underlying phenomenon is the new primary importance then assumed by the Scriptures. The names that became fashionable henceforth explicitly refer to Biblical characters, especially those constitutive of the national history and identity.[68]

---

[66]For Jaffa, see *CIJ*, II, 892-959, and S. Klein (ed.), *Sefer Hayishuv* I/1 (Jerusalem 1939, reprint Bialik Institute, 1978, in Hebrew), p. 80-89; for Beth-Shearim, *CIJ*, II, 993-1161 and, especially, M. Schwabe and B. Lifshitz, *Beth She'arim, II. The Greek Inscriptions* (Jerusalem, Isr. Expl. Soc., 1967). On the features of Jewish onomastics in the Late Empire, studied through Rabbinic sources, see S. Klein, "On names and nicknames," *Lešonenu* 1 (1929), p. 325-350 (in Hebrew), especially p. 325-329, quoting the remarks of the Sages on the fashion prevailing in their time. According to these sources, two hundred years after the destruction of the Temple, the most common names were those of the Patriarchs and of the eponyms of the first four tribes, Reuben, Simon, Levi and Judah. For the synagogal inscriptions from Palestine in Semitic languages, see the index of proper names in J. Naveh, *On Stone and Mosaic. The Aramaic and Hebrew Inscriptions from Ancient Synagogues* (Jerusalem, Isr. Expl. Soc., 1978); and its counterpart for Greek, Lea Roth-Gerson, *The Greek Inscriptions from the Synagogues in Eretz-Israel* (Jerusalem, Yad Y. Ben-Zvi, 1987), both in Hebrew. For the Sages, A. Hyman, *Toledot Hatannaïm ve-Ha'amoraïm* (Los Angeles, 1911, reprint Jerusalem, 1964); for the Mishnah alone, H. Duensing, *Verzeichnis der Personennamen und der geographischen Namen in der Mischna* (Stuttgart, W. Kohlhammer Verlag, 1960); Z. Frankel, *Mavo Hayerushalmi* (Breslau, 1870, reprint Jerusalem, 1964), p. 56-132, gives the lists of Palestinian Amoraim mentioned in both Talmuds.

[67]See in particular the publication of the great inscription from Aphrodisias in Caria by J. Reynolds and R. Tannenbaum, *Jews and Godfearers at Aphrodisias* (*Cambridge Philological Society, Supplementary Volume* 12, Cambridge Phil. Society, 1987), especially the remarks on personal names, p. 93-115. For Italy, see H.J. Leon, *The Jews of Ancient Rome* (Philadelphia, 1960), chap. 5.

[68]Besides the transformation of the onomastical stock, the new mood is also conspicuous in the trend of purism that affected the spelling of names already long-popular: in the Aramaic speaking area, *Yonathan* gave way to *Yehonathan*, and conversely *Yehosef* – an analogic form which came into fashion during the Hellenistic period – was replaced by the etymologically more correct *Yosef*: *Yôsef* is originally a hypocoristic form of *Yosefyah* (just as *Nathan* is short for *Yehonathan* or *Nathan'el*). But after the Persian period, as the process by which diminutives were created evolved, these names were perceived as secular ones. The form *Yehosef* stems from an analogy with *Yehonathan* and other theophoric names of the

In a pioneering study, L. Zunz had already noted, over a century and a half ago,[69] that the Hebrew names that are most typical today, those of Moses and his brother Aaron, those of the two kings David and Solomon, became common rather late, from the Late Empire or the Byzantine period onwards, if not during the Middle Ages. The much more abundant documentation available today leads us to qualify Zunz' statements (especially as far as the Patriarchs' names, which he puts on the same level as the four above mentioned, are concerned), but, on the whole, his conclusions remain valid.

As compared with the Late Empire, when the distinctive features took shape which for a long time were to characterize Jewish identity – that is, features typical of minority communities defining themselves in

---

same type (for a study of this phenomenon and the conclusions to be drawn from it, see T. Ilan, "On the different spellings of proper names during the Second Commonwealth," *Lešonenu* 52 [1988], p. 3-7, in Hebrew). The neo-classical spelling, aligned with the rules prevailing in the Bible and pervading also the texts of the Mishnah (whose manuscripts have undergone a thorough process of expurgation), is interestingly attested, as well, in the epigraphical material at Jaffa and Beth-Shearim, which is all the more striking as this kind of source normally reflects not scholarly but popular trends. In the same way, the influence of the Septuagint became pervasive in the Greek speaking world; Biblical names were now deprived of all Greek inflections: the *Iakoubis* and *Isakos* in the first two *CPJ* volumes become *Iakôb* and *Isak* in *CPJ*, III (although names featuring declensions may still be found even later: see Reynolds–Tannenbaum, *op. cit.*, p. 115, nn. 1 and 3). Several factors intervened in the new trend. The return to a classical way of writing began around the time when Hebrew was ceasing to be a living language, that is with the extinction of the survivors of the Bar-Kosiba revolt. Letters in Hebrew were indeed still found among the documents dating back to the revolt which were discovered in the caves of the Judaean desert (see Y.E. Kutscher, "The Language of the Hebraic and Aramaic Letters of Bar-Kosiba and his contemporaries. I. Aramaic Letters," *Lešonenu* 25 [1961], p. 117-134 and "II, Hebraic Letters," *ibidem* 26 [1962], p. 7-23 [in Hebrew]). Having been expelled from Judaea, the Jews of that region found themselves a minority in Galilee, where Hebrew was never the vernacular. (Actually, a similar shift occurred in 8th century Europe during the cultural renaissance under the Carolingians, which expressed itself in the return to a purified Latin grammar and morphology. The rediscovery of classical Latin had a twofold result, at the expense of the vulgar form: Latin started to become a dead language, and the Romance languages began to grow aware of themselves). The upheavals which had occurred in the situation of the Jews, whose communities were turning into minorities in their own land, were probably not alien to the process either. The shift to a form of name-giving bearing a clearer and clearer Biblical imprint reflects the need for Jews to assert their identity more sharply. Later, they may also have been subjected to the influence of the Christians, when the latter began taking Biblical names.

[69]L. Zunz, *Namen der Juden* (Leipzig, 1837, *Gesamte Schriften*, II, p. 1-82), quoted by V. Tcherikover, *The Jews in Egypt*, p. 180-181 and n. 1.

relation to the Scriptures – the use of Biblical names during the Graeco-Roman period remained profoundly marked by oral traditions and reactions to the surrounding historical context (as illustrated by the impact of the Maccabean revolt on Judaean onomastics). The Late Empire saw Palestinian Jews gradually aligning their behavior with that of their brethren living "outside of the Land," to use the Rabbinic phrase. This was due to the fact that Palestinian Jews were now as much a minority as the diaspora communities – which were now, in turn, deprived of the dynamic influence of a lively national center.

In contrast with this eventual uniformity, the previous period was characterized by two distinct situations, that of the national center and that of the groups of emigrés established in alien countries for several generations. The transformation of these groups into crystallized diasporas set the problem of their self-definition in new terms. We have already seen that the novel situation of the diaspora communities led to a distinctive behavior in terms of name-giving. The question we are now left with is whether the differences vis-à-vis Judaea involved only minor, quantitative transformations or whether their unusual position resulted in a qualitative modification of the very foundations of naming; in other words, whether this situation prompted alternative cultural references as the basis for the group's cohesion and self-definition.

5–Hebrew anthroponymy in Egypt: between scriptural reference and oral tradition

The appearance of Biblical anthroponymy can be observed as well in the Palestinian as in the Graeco-Egyptian documents. A closer study, however, will reveal perceptible differences between the two areas.

One of these differences is simply due to the linguistical substratum. In Egypt, the Biblical names (which, incidentally, adopt local inflections, -ις for masculine ones, *Iakoubis, Isakis, Iosepis,*[70] -ους for the feminine,

---

[70]The nominative forms *Isakis, Iôsêpis, Iakoubis,* and the like, that are common in Egypt as early as Hellenistic times, are to be distinguished from the similar forms of the Later Roman period. In the latter case, -ις results from a phonetical contraction for -ι<ο>ς, the genitive remaining the classical -ιου. In Egypt, we have to do with a so-called "Egyptianizing" declension because of its frequency in the local native anthroponymy, the genitive being -ιος, -ιδος or -ιτος (the latter seems to be specific to Egypt). Compare *P. Mich. Zen.,* I, 67 (παρὰ Ζαβδιτος), *CPJ,* I, 136, l. 3 (Ἀλέξανδρος Ἰσακιος). See F.T. Gignac, *A Grammar of the Greek Papyri of the Roman and Byzantine Periods, II. Morphology (Testi e documenti per lo studio dell'antichità,* 55a, Milano, Cisalpino-Goliardica, 1981), pp. 55-57 and 75. On the reduction of the final /io/ into /i/ in Asia Minor, where the process appears very early and has been best analyzed, see Cl. Brixhe, *Essai sur le grec anatolien au début de notre ère (Travaux et mémoires de l'Université de Nancy-II, Série Etudes anciennes, 1,*

Sambathous) gave birth to feminine derivations, like *Isakous*[71] from *Isakis*. Such a secondary creation is understandable only if the original meaning and even linguistical structure of *Yiṣḥaq* had been forgotten.[72]

More interesting is the difference which can be perceived in the attitude vis-à-vis the stock of Biblical names. T. Ilan remarks that, except for rare instances (such as the feminine use of the name Shelomṣion, formerly only masculine), we see no creation of new Hebrew names during the Graeco-Roman period, which fully confirms V. Tcherikover's views: only the Biblical stock was in use.

However, in Judaea, the relative popularity of a name is not to be explained solely by Biblical influence. Some of the most common names relate to a rather secondary Biblical character: thus, *Ishmael*, the name of Abraham's son by Hagar, was strikingly more widespread than that of his half-brother Isaac, patriarch of Israel.[73] This can only be understood if the proper names were inserted first and foremost into living oral tradition handed down in the families. As a matter of fact, the number of proper names that seem to owe their ascendancy directly to the Bible is relatively limited, especially considering the number of bearers involved.

This was not the same in Egypt. The names best illustrating the difference between Palestine and Egypt are those of the Patriarchs, Abraham, Isaac and Jacob. *Abraham* remained simply out of use in Palestine until a much later period (probably until about the fourth century CE) while, remarkably enough, one bearer is found in Egypt during Ptolemaic times already (*Abramos*, *CPJ*, I, 50) and six during Roman times (*Abramos, Abramis*).[74] We find nine occurrences of *Isaac* in

---

Nancy UP, 1984), pp. 49-50 and 67 (I thank Professor Thomas Drew-Bear for having drawn my attention to this book).

[71]*CPJ*, III, 455, l. 3, from 137 CE.

[72]Similar deformations proving that the etymology of names has been forgotten are attested also in Greek circles settled in the Latin speaking area. In a Greek family living in Lyons (*Année Épigraphique* 1961, no. 68 = P. Wuilleumier, *Inscriptions latines des trois Gaules* [Paris, 1963], p. 99-100, no. 251), *Daphniola*, from *Daphne*, was turned to *Danfiola* while the masculine *Danfius* had appeared. It can be infered from this "fact of language" that the family was ignorant of Greek: see Th. Drew-Bear, "Sur l'onomastique grecque de deux inscriptions à Lyon," in F. Bérard and Y. Le Bohec (eds.), *Inscriptions latines de Gaule Lyonnaise* (Collection du Centre d'Etudes Romaines et Gallo-Romaines, Université de Lyon-III, 10, Paris, De Boccard, 1992), p. 51-56, p. 51-52. This parallel proves clearly enough that it is not necessary to appeal to a Biblical inspiration to explain *Isakous*. The family tradition could have produced it.

[73]The example is borrowed from N.G. Cohen, "Jewish Names as Cultural Indicators in Antiquity," *Journal of Jewish Studies* 7 (1976), p. 97-128, p. 198.

[74]Concerning the specific case of *Abraham*, unused in Palestine while attested in Egypt, see already S. Klein, *Jüdisch-Palästinisches Corpus Inscriptionum (Ossuar-,*

Palestine, and as many in Egypt, three from the Ptolemaic (*Isakis*) and six from the Roman period (*Isakis, Eisakis*). *Jacob* is the only one to present a somewhat important distribution in Palestine, with thirty-four instances, while in Egypt it was one of the most common names, with four bearers identified in Hellenistic times (to the three *Iakoubis* of *CPJ*, add a *Iakkobios*, *CPR*, XIII, 21, col. II, l. 4) and twelve in Roman times (*Iakoubos, Iakôbos, Iakobos*). The disproportion between the two countries is all the more striking if one considers that the Palestinian sample includes some 2,000 male individuals, a name being defined as common by T. Ilan from forty bearers on. None of the Patriarchs' names reaches this threshold. In Egypt the sample is of course much narrower (a convenient source is still the prosopographical list appended to *CPJ*, III, though it would need to be updated and some doubtful cases should be excluded from it). It seems reasonable to consider a name common from eight or ten occurrences on. Two out of the three Patriarchs' names may thus be counted as such. This – still limited – comparison leads us to the conclusion that the Jews of Egypt were much fonder of prominent Biblical characters' names than their Palestinian brethren.

In all three cases, it seems indeed that only the scriptural references can be invoked to explain this popularity. The Jewish self-definition, understood here through anthroponymy, seems to have appealed more directly in Egypt to the religious factor, through the specific medium of the sacred text, in this case the Septuagint. But curiously enough, it seems that the influence of the Septuagint is to be restricted to the Patriarchs' names.

One might think that this influence would also have contributed to popularize the eponymous names of the twelve tribes. As a matter of fact, this does not seem to be the case, though observation is somewhat hindered by the scanty number of sources.

In Egypt, only three of the names of Jacob's twelve sons are presently attested, *Simon, Joseph* and *Judah* (we saw above what must be thought of the use of *Gad* by Jews). In Judaea, T. Ilan numbers at least three more: *Benjamin, Manasseh, Reuben.*[75] They remain relatively rare, however; given the disproportion between the samples (as we already noted, T. Ilan had access to nearly 2,000 male individuals, a figure we are very far

---

Grab- und Synagogen-Inschriften), (Wien-Berlin, 1920, reprint Hildesheim, Verlag Dr. H.A. Gerstenberg, 1971), no. 163.

[75]In her collection of data, T. Ilan numbers five occurrences of *Benjamin* (among which *t. Sheqalim*, 2:14, *CIJ* 1228), six of *Manasseh* (e.g. *AJ*, XII, 157, *BJ*, II, 567, *P. Murabb.*, 110), two of *Reuben* (*t. Shavuot*, 3:6 and *p. Kilayim*, IX, 4, p. 2c; see also N.G. Cohen, "Jewish Names as Cultural Indicators," [above, n. 73], p. 117-128). Note also two isolated instances, one of *Issachar* (*b. Pesahim*, 57a), the other of *Ephraim* (*b. Baba Metsia*, 87a).

from reaching in Egypt), it is impossible to determine whether the absence of these three names in the Graeco-Egyptian documentation reflects reality or is merely due to chance.

However, the conspicuous gap between the three eponymous names attested and those of the other tribes suggests that they do not owe their popularity directly to the memory of Jacob's sons. There must be another factor involved. The case of *Simon* is well known: it provided an almost perfect equivalent between a Hebrew and a Greek name. V. Tcherikover (*Prolegomena*, p. 30) sees in the particular predilection among the Egyptian Jews for the name *Iosephos* a feature of local nationalism, since it would have recalled Pharaoh's minister, whom the Jews would have been proud to evoke. As a matter of fact, *Yoseph* was no less common in Palestine around the same period, but the fact that Philo's description of Joseph at Pharaoh's side, in *De Iosepho*, is clearly inspired by the figure of the Prefect of Egypt at the emperor's side proves convincingly enough that the reference to the Biblical character must have lain behind the choice of the name.[76] Though it was the least common, *Judah* may have pleased the diaspora Jews by its very meaning, since it referred to the land of their fathers. Thus, each case lies on the borderline between scriptural inspiration and historical reality.[77]

Finally, the prevalence of several other names in Roman times cannot be explained simply by their connection with the Bible: *Joshua* (one instance for the Hellenistic period, seven for the Roman), *Eleazar/Eliezer* (one, then five). The corresponding Biblical characters did not attract any particular attention from exegetes such as Philo.

Conclusion

The documentary sources cast light on the gradual development of self-awareness among the Jews of Egypt. Jewish identity first of all asserted itself by a distinctive evolution within the society of Hellenes, of which the Jews were at the outset an integral part. At the end of this process, the dramatic changes introduced in the socio-juridical structure of Ptolemaic society by the Roman administration (which contained the seeds of the serious conflicts between Greeks and Jews in Alexandria during the years 38-41 CE) made the gap explicit by giving it a legal form:

---

[76]T. Ilan, "Names of the Hasmoneans," p. 238, table 1.

[77]Two names, unattested in Egypt until now, are somewhat more common in Palestine itself: *Levi* numbers eighteen bearers, *Menahem*, twenty-six (on the confusion of an Egyptian name with the Hebrew *Levi* in papyrological sources, see V. Tcherikover, Introduction to *CPJ*, I, p. xviii, n. 6).

as well known, the new situation was not willingly accepted by the Jews, who saw their status fall below that of the Greeks.[78]

This sense of identity which developed among Egyptian Jewry was the product of two opposite tendencies. First, the process cannot be understood independently of the continuing close ties between the Jews of Egypt and the "metropolis," either at an individual level (the pilgrimage to the Temple of Jerusalem, the movement of people as well as of ideas in both directions), or in the form of more collective and institutionalized exchanges (the yearly sending of the half-sheqel to the Temple, or the intervention of Ananias, the Jewish commander, to dissuade Cleopatra III from annexing Alexander Jannaeus' kingdom[79]). At a more theoretical and spiritual level, this relationship to the metropolis also pervades Philo's writings.

Thus, the evolution we have endeavored to trace in Egypt was certainly fostered by the events in Judaea (the Maccabean outbreak and the subsequent foundation of the Hasmonaean state[80]); but, on the other hand, the process cannot be entirely credited to external events. The Egyptian Jews were not mere nationals from Judaea transplanted to the banks of the Nile. In the course of this study, we have noted various adaptations to the immediate local context. The most popular names among Egyptian Jews were not those of the heroes of Judaea, the Maccabees, but those of local characters, like the Biblical Joseph. It may well be that the growing peculiarity of the Jews within the class of Hellenes was partly also the result of a local crisis. Is this crisis reflected in the legendary account which we find in *III Maccabees*? Did it occur in the wake of the troubles that followed the battle of Raphia?

These differences, resulting from the Jews' insertion into a local context different in Egypt than in Judaea, are after all to be expected. If they went no further, the mechanism of national awakening would be fundamentally identical in the two countries: a political crisis prompting a renewed self-definition. But perhaps another dimension should be added: the inner vitality of Egyptian Jewry – a vitality clearly evidenced by the intellectual brilliance of learned Judaeo-Hellenistic circles in Alexandria and their literary output. The primary condition for this literature had been the translation of the Torah into Greek, in the form of

---

[78]See V. Tcherikover, "The Decline of the Jewish Diaspora in Egypt in the Roman Period," *JJS* 14 (1963), p. 1-32; J. Mélèze-Modrzejewski, *Les Juifs d'Egypte* (above, n. 3), p. 131-135.

[79]See above, n. 34, esp. M. Stern quoted there.

[80]On the consequences of the Maccabean revolt for Egyptian Jewry, see U. Rappaport, "The Samaritan Sect in the Hellenistic Period," *Zion* 55 (1990), p. 373-396 (in Hebrew).

the Septuagint, which gave access to the ancestral law and history. Strikingly enough, even though its presence was not yet as pervasive as it would become later under the Late Empire, the Septuagint seems to have set a much clearer stamp on name-giving trends in Egypt than it did in Judaea around the same time: we have thus remarked on the conspicuous predilection for the three Patriarchs' names, *Abraham, Isaac* and *Jacob*.

It seems then that the reference to the homeland – references which have clearly a national character (though the religious is not entirely to be excluded, owing to the central status of the Temple), and which relate by definition to a center situated *outside* of the group affected by it – was partly replaced, or covered over, by an inner constitutive element. It would be useful, of course, to set this process in a closer chronological connection with the developing habit of Torah reading in the synagogues, whether in Alexandria or in the *chora*. We may at least ask ourselves whether, beyond the immediate political events that functioned as the necessary triggers, the spreading influence of the Septuagint throughout the country was not also the primary condition of the awakening of Jewish self-awareness, previously diluted in the relatively open melting pot of the community of Hellenes of the third century BCE. This might partly explain why (taking into account the limited sources available) the exact beginnings of the process remain hard to pinpoint.

Thus, the reference to the homeland gave way, in part, to an appeal not only to the particular history of the group, but also to its religious culture, through its scriptural medium. If this is the case, the process of Jewish self-definition in Egypt, involving the group's relation to the sacred Book, anticipated the mechanism which was to spread among all the Jewish communities by the second or third century CE.

As detected through the process of revival of national anthroponymy, more especially through the taste evinced for Biblical names, the Jews of Egypt have thus been imperceptibly moving from the situation of an ethnic group settled in an alien milieu to a diaspora community, drawing its vitality not only from its numerous relations with the "metropolis," but also from an inner strength. The shift moreover implied the growing awareness of a particularism, that is, the formation of a diaspora situation perceived as such. The difference between a community of emigrés and a community of diaspora lies in the self-perception of the group. It is not only a matter of historical, material reality: as far as their legal status was concerned, the Jews remained, to the very end of Graeco-Macedonian rule in Egypt, a mere component of the class of Hellenes. Given the organization of Ptolemaic society, they could not have been anything else. The notion of diaspora involves a dimension of mental representation.

The main interest of an onomastical study does not lie, of course, in its ability to *reveal* these features. The contemporary literature, as recent studies show[81], reflects just as much the way the Jews coped with the emergence of a new reality, the diaspora, and how they assimilated the perception of this reality. What the study of proper names reveals through the documentary sources of the *chora*, is that this vitality and self-awareness were not restricted to an intellectual elite, nor were they limited to Alexandria.

List of titles abbreviated in the footnotes

Benz: Fr. L. Benz, *Personal Names in the Phoenician and Punic Inscriptions. A Catalog, Grammatical Study and Glossary of Elements* (*Studia Pohl*, 8, Rome, Biblical Institute Press, 1972).

Bickerman, "Ezra–Nehemiah": E.J. Bickerman, "The Generation of Ezra and Nehemiah," *Proceedings of the American Academy for Jewish Research* 45 (1978), p. 1-28.

Cantineau: J. Cantineau, *Le Nabatéen. Choix de textes, lexique* (Paris, Leroux, 1932).

CIJ: J.-B. Frey, *Corpus Inscriptionum Judaicarum*, I-II (Vatican, 1936-52). New ed. CIJ I (New York, 1975), with a *Prolegomenon* by B. Lifshitz.

CPJ: V. Tcherikover, A. Fuks, *Corpus Papyrorum Judaicarum* I-III (Magnes Press, the Hebrew University of Jerusalem/Harvard UP, 1957-1964, with the collaboration of M. Stern and D.M. Lewis).

CPR, XIII: H. Harrauer, *Corpus Papyrorum Raineri*, XIII. *Neue Papyri zum Steuerwesen im 3. Jh. v. Chr.* (Wien, 1987).

CPR, XVIII: B. Kramer, *Corpus Papyrorum Raineri*, XVIII, *Griechische Texte* XIII. *Das Vertragsregister von Theogenis [P. Vindob. G 40618]*, (Wien, 1991).

Dizionario: A. Calderini, *Dizionario dei nomi geographici dell'Egitto greco-romano* (a cura di S. Daris, Milano, Cisalpino-Goliardica, 1935-1987).

Dura, V, 1: *The Excavations at Dura-Europos conducted by Yale University and the French Academy of Inscriptions and Letters, Final Report V Part I. The Parchments and Papyri*, by C.B. Welles, R.O. Fink and J.F. Gilliam (Yale UP, New Haven, 1959).

Fraser–Matthews, *Lexicon*: P.M. Fraser, E. Matthews, *A Lexicon of Greek Personal Names*, I. *The Aegean Islands. Cyprus. Cyrenaica* (The British Academy, Oxford Clarendon Press, 1987).

---

[81]For a literary approach to the phenomenon, see W.C. Van Unnik, *Das Selbstverständnis der jüdischen Diaspora in der hellenistisch-römischen Zeit* (*Arbeiten zur Geschichte des antiken Judentums und des Urchristentums*, 17, Leiden/New York/Cologne, E.J. Brill, 1993). See also, for a more general perspective, J.J. Collins, *Between Athens and Jerusalem. Jewish Identity in the Hellenistic Diaspora* (New York, Crossroad, 1983).

Hopfner: Th. Hopfner, "Graezierte, griechisch-ägyptische, bzw. ägyptisch-griechische und hybride theophore Personennamen aus Griechischen Texten, Inschriften, Papyri, Ostraka...," *Archiv Orientálni* 15 (1944), p. 1-64.

Ilan T., "Names of the Jews": Tal Ilan, "Names of the Jews in the Second Commonwealth. A Statistical Study," M.A. dissertation of the Hebrew University of Jerusalem, 1983 (unpublished, in Hebrew).

–, "Names of the Hasmoneans": Tal Ilan, "The Names of the Hasmoneans in the Second Temple Period," *Eretz-Israel* 19 (Avi-Yonah Volume, Jerusalem, 1987), p. 238-241 (in Hebrew).

Namenbuch: Fr. Preisigke, *Namenbuch enthaltend alle griechischen, lateinischen, ägyptischen, hebräischen, arabischen und sonstigen semitischen und nichtsemitischen Menschennamen, soweit sie in griechischen Urkunden (Papyri, Ostraka, Inschriften, Mumienschilder usw.) Ägyptens sich vorfinden* (Heidelberg, 1922, reprint Amsterdam, 1967).

Onomasticon: D. Foraboschi, *Onomasticon alterum papyrologicum* (Milano, 1968-71).

P. Cair. Zen.: Zenon Papyri, *Catalogue général des antiquités égyptiennes du Musée du Caire,* I-V, ed. C.C. Edgar (Cairo, 1925-1940).

Peters–Thiersch, *Marissa:* J.P. Peters, H. Thiersch, *Painted Tombs in the Necropolis of Marissa (Marêshah),* (Palestine Expl. Fund, London, 1905. The inscriptions were published anew in *SEG XXXIV,* [1984], nos. 1477-1502).

P. Murabb.: Discoveries in the Judaean Desert, II. Les Grottes de Murabba'ât (eds. P. Benoît, J. T. Milik et R. de Vaux, Oxford Clarendon Press, 1961).

P. Petrie: The Flinders Petrie Papyri, I-II, ed. J.P. Mahaffy and III, eds. J.P. Mahaffy and J.G. Smyly (Dublin, 1891-1905).

P. Petrie²: The Petrie Papyri, Second Edition, I. *The Wills,* ed. W. Clarysse (*Collectanea Hellenistica,* 2, Bruxelles, 1991).

SEG: Supplementum Epigraphicum Graecum (Amsterdam, J.C. Gieben).

Select Papyri: A.S. Hunt and C.C. Edgar (eds.), *Select Papyri,* I-II (Loeb Classical Library).

Stark: J.K. Stark, *Personal Names in Palmyrene Inscriptions* (Oxford Clarendon Press, 1971).

V. Tcherikover, *Prolegomena:* CPJ, I, p. 1-111.

–, *The Jews in Egypt:* V. Tcherikover, *The Jews in Egypt in the Hellenistic-Roman Age in the Light of the Papyri* (2nd revised edition, Jerusalem, Magnes Press, The Hebrew University, 1963), (in Hebrew, with an English summary).

W. Chr.: L. Mitteis and U. Wilcken, *Grundzüge und Chrestomathie der Papyruskunde,* I-II (Leipzig/Berlin, 1912).

Index

Brown Judaic Studies

140261	*The Talmud of Babylonia: An American Translation XIII.D: Tractate Yebamot Chapters 10-16*	Jacob Neusner
140262	*The Talmud of Babylonia: An American Translation XV. A: Tractate Nedarim Chapters 1-4*	Jacob Neusner
140263	*The Talmud of Babylonia: An American Translation XV.B: Tractate Nedarim Chapters 5-11*	Jacob Neusner
140264	*Studia Philonica Annual 1992*	David T. Runia
140265	*The Talmud of Babylonia: An American Translation XVIII.A: Tractate Gittin Chapters 1-3*	Jacob Neusner
140266	*The Talmud of Babylonia: An American Translation XVIII.B: Tractate Gittin Chapters 4 and 5*	Jacob Neusner
140267	*The Talmud of Babylonia: An American Translation XIX.A: Tractate Qiddushin Chapter 1*	Jacob Neusner
140268	*The Talmud of Babylonia: An American Translation XIX.B: Tractate Qiddushin Chapters 2-4*	Jacob Neusner
140269	*The Talmud of Babylonia: An American Translation XVIII.C: Tractate Gittin Chapters 6-9*	Jacob Neusner
140270	*The Talmud of Babylonia: An American Translation II.A: Tractate Shabbat Chapters 1 and 2*	Jacob Neusner
140271	*The Theology of Nahmanides Systematically Presented*	David Novak
140272	*The Talmud of Babylonia: An American Translation II.B: Tractate Shabbat Chapters 3-6*	Jacob Neusner
140273	*The Talmud of Babylonia: An American Translation II.C: Tractate Shabbat Chapters 7-10*	Jacob Neusner
140274	*The Talmud of Babylonia: An American Translation II.D: Tractate Shabbat Chapters 11-17*	Jacob Neusner
140275	*The Talmud of Babylonia: An American Translation II.E: Tractate Shabbat Chapters 18-24*	Jacob Neusner
140276	*The Talmud of Babylonia: An American Translation III.A: Tractate Erubin Chapters 1 and 2*	Jacob Neusner
140277	*The Talmud of Babylonia: An American Translation III.B: Tractate Erubin Chapters 3 and 4*	Jacob Neusner
140278	*The Talmud of Babylonia: An American Translation III.C: Tractate Erubin Chapters 5 and 6*	Jacob Neusner
140279	*The Talmud of Babylonia: An American Translation III.D: Tractate Erubin Chapters 7-10*	Jacob Neusner
140280	*The Talmud of Babylonia: An American Translation XII: Tractate Hagigah*	Jacob Neusner
140281	*The Talmud of Babylonia: An American Translation IV.A: Tractate Pesahim Chapter I*	Jacob Neusner
140282	*The Talmud of Babylonia: An American Translation IV.B: Tractate Pesahim Chapters 2 and 3*	Jacob Neusner
140283	*The Talmud of Babylonia: An American Translation IV.C: Tractate Pesahim Chapters 4-6*	Jacob Neusner
140284	*The Talmud of Babylonia: An American Translation IV.D: Tractate Pesahim Chapters 7 and 8*	Jacob Neusner
140285	*The Talmud of Babylonia: An American Translation IV.E: Tractate Pesahim Chapters 9 and 10*	Jacob Neusner
140286	*From Christianity to Gnosis and From Gnosis to Christianity*	Jean Magne
140287	*Studia Philonica Annual 1993*	David T. Runia
140288	*Diasporas in Antiquity*	Shaye J. D. Cohen, Ernest S. Frerichs
140289	*The Jewish Family in Antiquity*	Shaye J. D. Cohen

Brown Studies on Jews and Their Societies

Brown Studies in Religion